Viet

The Price of Peace

Contents

Acknowledgements

Some material in this book is base... report for Oxfam written by Larry Jaga... Advice and valuable information was provided by Ben Fawcett.

Designed by Oxfam Design Department OX182
Printed by Oxfam Print Unit. Published by O...
274 Banbury Road Oxford OX2 7DZ
ISBN 0-85598-152-0

Chris Brazier

BEN FAWCETT

Introduction

VIETNAM: a nightmare land where American boy soldiers were assailed by faceless, ruthless guerillas; a symbol of hardline Communism, where the Party brooks no dissent and cuts itself off from the mainstream of the world; a country so forbidding that thousands of 'boat people' have risked their lives in flimsy craft on the open seas to escape it.

These are the standard images of Vietnam which most people in the West carry in their minds. Anyone who had actually been there, however, would carry back with them an entirely different set of impressions.

Vietnam: a land of quite staggering beauty. The luminous green of the paddy fields in the Red River Delta, where conical-hatted farmers stoop to their timeless, back-breaking labour. The spectacular coastline and long white beaches around Danang and Nha Trang, untouched by the tourist hordes that have poured into other coastal areas of South-East Asia. Ha Long Bay, with brown-sailed junks serene against a backdrop of hills that interlock and counterpoint in delicate shades of grey and green, the farthest ones gently merging with a misty sky.

Vietnam: a country that fought bravely for its independence throughout four decades against the Japanese, the French, and finally against the Americans. It still bears the scars of the last of those wars: in the military debris littering its parks and roadsides, the unexploded mines which continue to kill or maim unsuspecting peasants; in an environment ravaged by the spraying of defoliating chemicals like Agent Orange, from the effects of which whole regions struggle to recover; and, most important of all, in its enforced isolation from the rest of the world, from the trade and aid that would have allowed it to recover from the rigours of war and make a fresh start.

Vietnam: an economy which has thrown off its 'Marxist-Leninist' straitjacket and tried to adjust to the free market, with almost no help from Western powers, who have rewarded other converts such as China, the Soviet Union and Poland. A former importer of food which is now one of the world's leading exporters of rice. A Communist country that sees arch-capitalists like South Korea as potential models.

Yet even these alternative images are not enough to give a full sense of the modern Vietnam. The best place to start is with the people. The world still sees the Vietnamese as hostile, a legacy of the US-Vietnam War. It is hardly surprising that young American soldiers, caught in a maze of paddy fields and jungles, wondering where the next guerilla attack would come from, seeing every local as a potential enemy, should have conceived of the Vietnamese as threatening. But the present-day reality is far from that grim stereotype.

The Vietnamese have much in common with other Asian peoples. They value dignity and hard work. They have a strong sense of pride in their own 5,000-year history and independent cultural traditions. And, despite the Stalinist years when petty commerce was forbidden, they are natural entrepreneurs: whereas ten years

KEITH BERNSTEIN

Above: Pedal power in Hanoi. Cars are still something of a rarity; bicycles are the best way to get around.

Wet earth, wide sky. Morning in the Mekong Delta - time of the hardest work in the rice fields.

ago Hanoi's streets were lifeless and drab, the narrow streets north of Hoan Kiem Lake are now a riot of colour and commercial bustle.

But what sets the Vietnamese apart is their history of suffering and the awesomely generous way in which they deal with that legacy. In adversity they have always knuckled down to the task at hand, just as the peasant farmers, who make up the vast majority of the population, have always stoically endured the impact of typhoon or flood. But after such a catastrophe as the long war with the United States, you would expect to find a well of bitterness – particularly since that war has been continued relentlessly by other, economic, means.

Instead, Western visitors to Vietnam are usually humbled by the warmth with which they are received. Again and again, ordinary Vietnamese people – even those who lost children or spouses in the conflict – will tell you that all they want is to be left alone to live in peace. As you travel through the country from the northern hills to the Mekong Delta in the south, people in the fields and streets convince you that their dearest wish is to open up to the world – to make friends even of those who still regard them as enemies.

CHRIS BRAZIER

Geography

Vietnam lies in mainland South-East Asia, forming a long 'S' along more than 1600 kilometres (1000 miles) of the eastern coast of Indochina. The maximum width, in the north bordering China, is 600 kilometres; but in the central region the country is only 50 kilometres wide.

A mountain range, the Truong Son, runs down the whole length of the country, dividing it from its western neighbours, Laos and

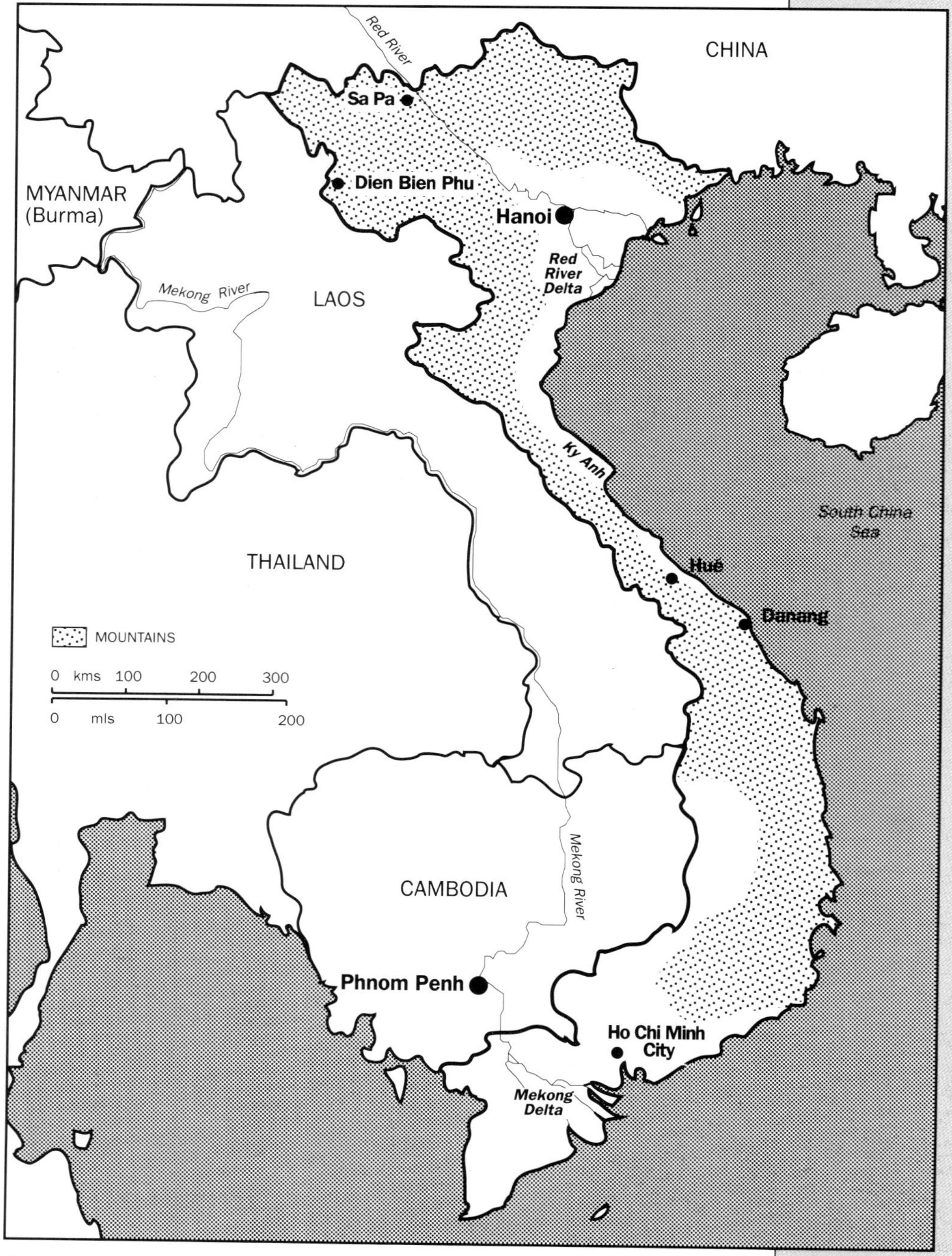

BEN FAWCETT

KEITH BERNSTEIN

***Bottom:* Where the mountains meet the sea, in Vietnam's narrow central provinces.**

Cambodia. The mountains run down to the coast of the South China Sea in a series of spurs, in the narrow central region, cutting off small coastal plains. Two low-lying Deltas – in the north the Red River, and in the south, the Mekong – provide the agricultural centres of Vietnam.

The south of Vietnam is in the humid tropics, and is subject to two monsoons – the south-west monsoon from May to October and the north-east from November to April. The former brings tropical storms from the south Pacific, which batter the coastline every year. Most parts of the country enjoy relatively abundant rainfall, which sometimes leads to flooding in the river Deltas. The farming land is protected by huge networks of earth dykes, and land is continuously being reclaimed. However, in certain areas the rainfall can be erratic and there are periods of drought.

Near Sa Pa, in the far north of the country. The terracing is hundreds of years old.

The climate varies from humid tropical conditions in the south to temperate in the northern hills. During the winter, freezing polar winds blow over northern Vietnam, bringing January temperatures as low as 10°C in Hanoi. But the summers are hot and very humid, and in July the temperature averages 30°C. The Mekong Delta experiences less variable weather conditions, with a mean annual temperature of 27°C.

With a total population of over 67 million, pressure on the available land is intense. The mass of the population is still dependent on agriculture. With an average population density of over 200 people per square kilometre, Vietnam is second only to Bangladesh in terms of farming population per hectare of cultivated land. In some provinces of the Red River Delta the density reaches 1000 per square kilometre. Only 9 million of the country's 33 million hectares are under cultivation, and only 7.1 million hectares are under food crops. This results in an average of only a little over 1,000 square metres per capita of arable land. The Government hopes to bring a further 2.8 million hectares into production by the end of the century as a result of irrigation and drainage schemes. The comprehensive plan centres on the Red River and its tributaries. However, Vietnam's agricultural land is threatened by soil erosion, partly caused by deforestation, and a loss of fertility because of over-cultivation.

Rice is the major crop, grown throughout Vietnam with the main production area in the

Mekong Delta. Some experts maintain that this fertile region could produce enough rice to feed the whole of the country, given adequate investment in irrigation schemes and improved agricultural technology. At present, only 32 per cent of the arable land is irrigated.

Besides its fertile agricultural land, Vietnam's other great assets are its mineral deposits. There are major coal reserves, of high-quality anthracite, particularly in the northern coastal province of Quang Ninh. Coal production at present levels could continue for over 400 years. Oil and gas reserves, including offshore fields, are now being explored and production is increasing rapidly with significant foreign investment. Important quantities of bauxite, iron ore and apatite (used for production of phosphate fertilisers) are known to exist. Other smaller amounts of rare minerals – gold, nickel, mercury – occur but none as yet are fully exploited. Vietnam is endowed with a rich potential and an economically strategic location in a vibrant part of the world.

Facts and figures

Land area:	330,363 sq km (1.4 x the size of UK)
Cultivated area:	89,833 sq km (27%) [Food crops: 70,911 sq km (21%)]
Population (1991):	67 million (UK 57.1 million) : 49.6% under 20 years old
Population growth:	2.1% per year (1979-89)
Population density:	203 / sq km
Life expectancy:	62 years (1988) (UK 75)
Urban population:	20% of total (UK 92%) Hanoi: 3.1 million (1989) Ho Chi Minh City: 3.9 million (1989) Haiphong: 1.4 million (1989)
Ethnic groups:	Kinh (lowland Vietnamese) 87%, Tay 1.8%, Thai 1.6%, Hoa (ethnic Chinese) 1.4%, Khmer 1.4%, 49 other groups 6.8%
Income per person:	US$150-200 (UK $10,420)
Occupations:	Agriculture/forestry/fishing: 72%, Industry: 14%, Trade and supply: 6%, Administration and service: 8%
Adult literacy rate:	82%; Male 88%, Female 80%.
Health:	Infant mortality (under 1 yr): 45-50/1000; 3.6 doctors per 10,000 population (UK 15/10,000)
Basic foods:	Rice – average consumption 0.46 kg/day
Main exports:	Rice, timber, coal, coffee, rubber, crude oil
Main imports:	Oil products, fertilisers
Currency:	Dong, early 1992 US$1 = about 11,000 Dong

Sources: Sample results of 1989 Vietnam Census; *The Situation of Women and Children*, UNICEF 1990; *Report on the Economy of Vietnam*, UNDP 1990; Economist Intelligence Unit; *Statistical data of the SR Vietnam* 1976-89.

History

'Vietnam has always been one country, one people,' says General Vo Nguyen Giap, who commanded the Vietnamese liberation army against first the French and then the Americans. 'Vietnamese history has been a long struggle for independence, self-determination and the unification of the Vietnamese people. And this struggle continues today, although now it is the feudalist ideas of the past against which we must fight.'

When the Chinese conquered the Red River Delta region of northern Vietnam in the second century BC, they found a feudal society practising wet-rice agriculture and engaging in some foreign trade. The Chinese introduced a centralised state and transplanted into it much of their Confucianist ideology. There were several serious rebellions against Chinese rule, including that led by the Trung sisters in AD 39, which saw them hold out for two years before drowning themselves in order to avoid capture. It was only a little over a thousand years ago that the Vietnamese, under Ngo Quyen, finally regained control of their own land.

Over the next 500 years they gradually extended their control

TRICIA PARKER

Early History (BC to 1954)

2879 BC:	Legendary founding of Vietnam by Hung Vuong
207 BC:	General Trieu Da combines the Red River Delta into Nam Viet under the Chinese Han dynasty
AD 39:	Trung sisters rebel against Chinese rule
939:	Ngo Quyen establishes an independent Vietnamese kingdom
1257-87:	Mongol invasions repelled
1407-27:	Further Chinese occupation
1471:	Champa Kingdom overcome
1558-1772:	Country divided between Trinh and Nguyen families (North and South)
1627:	Jesuit missionary Alexandre de Rhodes arrives in Hanoi
1771:	Tay Son Rebellion
1802:	Nguyen Anh defeats Tay Son forces and rules as Emperor Gia Long, from Hué
1858-9:	French forces seize Danang and Saigon
1874:	Franco-Vietnamese Treaty confirms French sovereignty over Cochinchina (southern Vietnam)
1883:	Harmond Convention establishes French protectorates in Annam and Tonkin (central and northern Vietnam)
19 May 1890:	Ho Chi Minh born
February 1930:	Vietnamese Communist Party founded
1940-45:	Vietnam occupied by Japan
1941:	Viet Minh founded in the northern mountains of Viet Bac
1944-45:	Famine in Annam and Tonkin causes 1.5-2 million deaths
Late August 1945:	August Revolution led by the Viet Minh
28 August 1945:	Democratic Republic of Vietnam (DRV) declared, with Ho Chi Minh as President
2 September 1945:	Ho Chi Minh declares Vietnamese independence in Ba Dinh Square, Hanoi
1945-54:	First Indochina War – against French domination
7 May 1954:	French surrender at Dien Bien Phu

Opera House, Hanoi. The French influence on the architecture is clear.

southwards at the expense of the Indianised Kingdom of Champa and the Khmer empire, which included the Mekong Delta. In the north there were many battles with the Chinese, and the Mongol invasions of the thirteenth century, led by Kublai Khan, were repulsed with the kind of determination the Americans were to encounter 700 years later. There were also battles against Chinese influence in the cultural sphere – particularly in the fields of law, literature and religion.

Then came a period of fragmentation, with rival dynasties in north and south sparring with each other over two centuries. When lasting union came it was under the emperor Gia Long in 1802 – and he owed his success to assistance from the French.

French traders and missionaries had already developed extensive contacts throughout the south of the country and the emperor became worried by their growing influence. The previous policies of granting trade concessions and tolerating Christian missionaries were reversed – and thereby provoked an official reaction in a France anxious to counter British influence in the region.

On 31 August 1858 a French naval squadron attacked Danang, unleashing a colonial war of conquest. The French Navy seized Saigon in 1861 and the rest of the Mekong Delta in 1867, creating the colony of Cochinchina. Within two decades the rest of Vietnam had been subdued too, though the emperors were kept as puppet figureheads. In 1887 French Indochina was formed from the colony of Cochinchina and the protectorates of Annam (central Vietnam), Tonkin (northern Vietnam), Cambodia and Laos.

The French justified their rule by the idea that they were bringing 'into light and liberty the races and peoples still enslaved by ignorance and despotism'. In reality, Vietnam was treated as a huge plantation fuelling French industrialisation. Many thousands of Vietnamese died labouring in appalling conditions on rubber plantations; rice was exported despite the fact that local people were starving.

Trieu Au, the Vietnamese equivalent of Joan of Arc, fought for Vietnam's independence against China in the third century AD. She is still worshipped as a sacred figure.

There was considerable resistance to French rule throughout Vietnam. The long tradition of opposing foreign occupation helped sustain strong independence sentiments. The Can Vuong (Aid the King) movement, which reached its peak in the 1880s, was led by mandarins who left the court rather than collaborate with the French. A new form of resistance emerged in the 1920s under the leadership of nationalists and Trotskyists – and later under the auspices of the Communist Party, formed by the exiled Ho Chi Minh in 1930.

The French were relieved of power in Indochina by Japan during the Second World War – but were left in administrative control because they collaborated with the Vichy regime in Paris.

Ho Chi Minh arrived back in Vietnam in February 1941, after an absence of 30 years, to lead the struggle against the Japanese and the French. He made the mountainous north his base and took the Communist Party into a strategic alliance, the Vietnam Independence League or Viet Minh, which it soon dominated. With US logistical support the Viet Minh continued to fight the Japanese until 1945 – at which point they marched into Hanoi and declared the independence of the Democratic Republic of Vietnam. However, no sooner was the Second World War over than the French attacked the Viet Minh, helped in the South by the British, who had been given temporary responsibility for the region and believed the former colonial authority should be restored. The French return forced the Viet Minh back into the hills and a long war ensued – the first Indochina War lasted nearly nine years. Ho Chi Minh's guerillas were backed after 1949 by newly-Communist China, while the French war effort was paid for by a US now agonising about Communist expansion.

Frustrated that guerilla warfare never allowed them to use their superior firepower, the French decided in 1954 to lure the Viet Minh into a battle at Dien Bien Phu, a valley near the Laotian border. But the Viet Minh mobilised an army twice as big as expected, and hauled heavy artillery to the top of the steep hills surrounding the valley, something the French had considered impossible. After 55 days of intense bombardment, Viet Minh troops over-ran Dien Bien Phu and the French colonial period was over.

Ho Chi Minh

Ho Chi Minh is one of the key figures of the twentieth century. The first President of an independent Vietnam, he led the resistance to the French, Japanese and Americans, and is still considered the father of the nation, referred to affectionately, even by opponents of Communism, as Bac Ho ('Uncle Ho').

Born Nguyen Sinh Cung in 1890, in Nghe An, Vietnam's poorest province, Ho left the country at the age of 21 as a galley boy on a French freighter. After three years at sea he worked as a cook in New York and London, beginning a lifetime habit of changing his name to mark each new phase. In London he was Nguyen Tat Thanh, but in Paris, where he spent six years, he marked a new political commitment by calling himself Nguyen Ai Quoc ('Nguyen the Patriot'). He joined the Communist Party and travelled to Moscow in 1924, where he was known as Comrade Linh; and from this point onwards, Ho's life was completely dedicated to freeing Vietnam from colonial rule.

In Canton, for the next three years he was Ly Thuy, a mobiliser of Vietnamese students, while in 1928 he was with Vietnamese dissidents in Thailand, shaven-headed and wearing the saffron robes of a Buddhist monk, and using the name Thau Chin. In 1930 he assembled rival factions in Hong Kong and launched the Vietnamese Communist Party. He was arrested and imprisoned, but escaped by persuading a guard to report him dead.

He spent the 1930s drifting between China and the Soviet Union, awaiting the right moment. It was a lonely life, dedicated to a dream distant in both geography and time. He was once found on a bridge over the Seine in Paris musing on what might have been: 'I always thought I would become a scholar or a writer, but I've

The idealised image of Ho Chi Minh still presides over public places and private homes alike.

become a professional revolutionary. I travel through many countries, but I see nothing.'

The Second World War brought him back to his homeland, to a base in the hills near the Chinese border, and it was from here that he marched south with the Viet Minh to take Hanoi and declare Vietnam an independent republic. His own Declaration of Independence deliberately echoed that of the United States: 'We hold the truth that all men are created equal, that they are endowed by their Creator with certain inalienable rights, among them life, liberty, and the pursuit of happiness'. Ho was hoping specifically for US support in his anti-colonial battle; but the choice of words is clear evidence that he was always first a nationalist and only second a communist. Ho's own most famous quotation underlines this further: 'There is nothing more precious than independence and freedom'.

Ho Chi Minh's last two and a half decades were dedicated to leading his people to unified independence, through the struggles of the Viet Minh against the French, and the Viet Cong against first the southern regime of Diem and then Thieu and the Americans. He died in 1969, six years before his dream of a unified, independent Vietnam was to become reality.

Much of the enduring respect for Ho in Vietnam derives from his personal qualities rather than his policies, from the sense that he was utterly and incorruptibly dedicated to his nation and his people. Throughout his life he was unpretentious and ascetic, shunning personal comfort – when he became President he refused to use the palace offered him and lived instead in a modest house in the grounds. As a result, he is still revered even by trenchant critics of Communism and the current Government. He would have regarded that as an infinitely more meaningful tribute than the cold and echoing halls of the Ho Chi Minh mausoleum and museum in Hanoi.

BEN FAWCETT

Ho Chi Minh Mausoleum, Hanoi.

The American War

JACQUES DANOIS/UNICEF

The victory of the Chinese Communists in 1949 transformed the French-Indochina War from a colonial struggle into an anti-communist crusade. Over the subsequent quarter of a century, the United States committed itself militarily and politically to maintaining anti-communist regimes throughout the region. The fact that these regimes were neither representative nor elected, that they were generally corrupt and extremely repressive, made no difference. The US was committed to propping up any regime in Asia which purported to be anti-communist.

The 1954 Geneva Conference divided Vietnam temporarily in two at the 17th parallel: a Communist North led by Ho Chi Minh and a South led by Ngo Dinh Diem. The Conference specified that free elections were to be held before 1956 and the country reunited. But the United States never ratified the agreement. President Eisenhower said in his memoirs: 'I have never talked... with a person knowledgeable in Indochinese affairs who did not agree that had the elections been held... 80 per cent of the population would have voted for Ho Chi Minh'.

Elections were ruled out, and the US began bolstering up the Diem regime in South Vietnam, which tortured and executed thousands of Viet Minh supporters. The Communists did not respond until 1960, when a new patriotic movement – the National Liberation Front – rallied all Diem's opponents in South Vietnam. A new war had begun.

Under President Kennedy, US involvement mounted steadily. American military 'advisers' regularly went into combat and on bombing missions. But their disenchantment with the corruption and incompetence of the Diem regime increased. In 1963, Diem and his brother Nhu launched a vicious repression of Buddhists, and the world was shocked by the protest of a monk who set himself on fire. The US backed a coup by dissatisfied generals, who assassinated both Diem and Nhu.

Conflict escalated. The North despatched troops covertly into the South down the 'Ho Chi Minh Trail'

Recent History (1954-1991)

21 July 1954:	**Geneva Agreements adopted, dividing Vietnam at the 17th Parallel**
1955:	**American advisers start training South Vietnamese troops**
October 1955:	**Republic of Vietnam established in the South under President Diem**
November 1963:	**Diem assassinated**
7 August 1964:	**US Congress adopts 'Gulf of Tonkin Resolution' giving the President power to authorise the use of force in Vietnam**
7 February 1965:	**US starts Operation Rolling Thunder, bombing the DRV**
9 March 1965:	**US ground troops land in Danang**
30-31 January 1968:	**'Tet Offensive': Communist troops occupy the American Embassy in Saigon and take over Hué for nearly a month**
January 1969:	**Peace talks begin in Paris**
May 1969:	**US troop strength peaks at 543,000**
10 June 1969:	**Provisional Revolutionary Government (PRG) of South Vietnam formed**
3 September 1969:	**Ho Chi Minh dies**
1969:	**Secret American bombing of 'Vietnamese sanctuaries' in Cambodia begins**
December 1972:	**'Christmas bombing' of Hanoi and Haiphong**
27 January 1973:	**Signature of the Paris Agreement on Ending the War**
29 March 1973:	**Last US combat troops leave Vietnam**
9 March 1975:	**People's Army of Vietnam launches the final offensive**

through the mountains. In 1965, President Johnson began the sustained bombing of North Vietnam, and the first marines arrived in Danang. By the end of that year there were 200,000 US soldiers in Vietnam; by the end of 1966 there were 400,000.

But it was not a war to their taste. The guerillas would strike and then disappear into vast networks of underground tunnels, or blend into the local community, where they had a good deal of popular support. Instead of using their superior firepower, US soldiers were eternally on patrol wondering when the next mine or booby trap would strike. Too often, they responded by treating any Vietnamese villager as a threat to be 'liquidated'. Civilian casualties were high; at least 25,000 civilians were killed and 50,000 more injured every year.

Children from a Buddhist orphanage play with detonated rockets, back in 1972.

On the eve of Tet (the Lunar New Year) in 1968, the North launched a major attack intended to liberate South Vietnam before the ailing Ho Chi Minh died. In the short term it failed: nowhere did the local population rise up in support, and the northern troops suffered devastating losses. But the Tet Offensive was a long-term success; television coverage of it profoundly shocked a US public which had been told everything was under control. Instead, they saw the Communist flag raised over Hué and the US Embassy in Saigon attacked. The anti-war movement in America gathered momentum, and the will to fight began to evaporate.

The new US President, Richard Nixon, spread the war into Cambodia – the murderous Khmer Rouge ultimately came to power as a result – but also started disengaging from Vietnam. US forces were steadily reduced and a peace agreement was eventually signed on 27 January 1973, after the destructive Christmas bombing campaign. The Americans withdrew as planned within 60 days, but both Vietnamese armies carried on fighting.

The US withdrawal devastated South Vietnam's economy. The North launched another major offensive on 10 March 1975 and routed their demoralised opponents; on 30 April Saigon fell and Vietnam was reunited.

17 April 1975:	**Khmer Rouge takes power in Cambodia**
30 April 1975:	**Saigon surrenders**
2 July 1976:	**Socialist Republic of Vietnam declared**
1977 - 78:	**Khmer Rouge launches frequent attacks on southern provinces**
29 June 1978:	**Vietnam admitted to Council for Mutual Economic Assistance (CMEA – association of communist countries)**
3 November 1978:	**Vietnam signs a 30-year Treaty of Friendship and Co-operation with the Soviet Union**
21 December 1978:	**Vietnamese forces invade Cambodia**
7 January 1979:	**Pol Pot's Khmer Rouge Government overthrown and the People's Republic of Cambodia established**
	Embargo on trade and aid imposed by the US
17 February - 5 March 1979:	**Chinese retaliatory invasion of northern provinces of Vietnam**
December 1986:	**Sixth Party Congress launches major economic reforms**
Early 1988:	**Serious food shortages in northern provinces**
April 1988:	**Resolution 10 on agricultural and other reforms adopted**
1989:	**Vietnam exports 1.5 million tons of rice**
September 1989:	**Remaining Vietnamese troops withdrawn from Cambodia**
June 1991:	**Seventh Party Congress confirms continued reforms**
October 1991:	**Cambodian peace accord signed. US announces it is ready to talk about resuming relations with Vietnam.**

One country, two peoples

Two Vietnamese win $100 in a lottery: the northerner spends the money on a new roof; the southerner on a television. Stories illustrating the difference between people from two distinct regions in the same country are common throughout the world – as between the North and South of England. In Vietnam such stories are politically sensitive – the whole independence struggle was, after all, founded on the belief that Vietnam is one country, one people. But the differences remain.

There is a difference in climate, for a start – the South is warm and humid all the year round whereas the North has distinct seasons. But there is an even more vital difference in cultural heritage: the North was ruled directly by China for over a thousand years and imbibed its strict, disciplined Confucian traditions; while the South was long part of the Champa kingdom which had Malay origins and a looser, Hindu philosophy. The Kinh people moved south as pioneers, expanding their frontier and gradually taking control of the land.

But the most important difference is a much more recent one, stemming from the fact that the country was split in two between 1954 and 1975. The North observed a strict communist system which was all the more austere because of its total dedication to winning the war. Private commerce was forbidden and all economic activity was subject to central planning, with Five Year Plans on the Stalinist model.

The South, meanwhile, was flooded with American money. At first, this money was simply pumped into the economy to bolster up the anti-communist regime and its military effort. But as American soldiers started to arrive en masse, so the South Vietnamese economy had to evolve to service them. People flocked to the cities, partly because the countryside had become a war zone, but also to take advantage of entirely new financial opportunities, whether as street traders, or as prostitutes. Between 1960 and 1974, the proportion of the workforce employed in agriculture dropped from 88 per cent to 55 per cent and the population of Danang grew from 50,000 to 500,000.

Not all southerners welcomed the American invasion, of course; besides those who joined the Viet Cong and fought actively against them, there were plenty of tacit Viet Cong sympathisers, passive resisters, and people who simply resented their country being taken over by a foreign power.

All the same, when North Vietnamese soldiers first marched into Saigon in 1975, they could hardly believe the luxuries that its citizens had enjoyed as part of their everyday

CHRIS BRAZIER

Stilt houses on the Saigon River.

CHRIS BRAZIER

life – wide avenues filled with Japanese cars, modern apartment buildings and expensive hotels, bars and restaurants blaring pop music, blue jeans and floppy hats, and expensive cosmetics. Northerners, motivated by slogans of independence and socialism, had sacrificed even the most basic amenities in order to help the war effort.

After the war was over, fashions and goods and even a whole life style began to filter slowly from the South to the North. From the early 1980s, people wearing baseball caps, bell-bottomed trousers and colourful clothes were seen on the streets of Hanoi. Then came the private coffee bars, with Western music, videos and imported beers. Gradually, the socialism of the North came to be seen by many as a lost cause, full of empty promises, leading nowhere. The free-market economics and consumerism of the war-time South became symbols of the hope for a better future. Although the South lost the war, it appears to have won the cultural peace.

When the Communist Hanoi Government took control of the whole country, there was bound to be a certain amount of discrimination against people who had been on the opposite side in the civil war. But the Communist Government also made the mistake of trying to squeeze this sprawling, artificially wealthy southern economy into the same mould as the North. This caused great resentment and, as a consequence, you can wander around the streets of Saigon (the imposition of the name Ho Chi Minh City is still resisted and resented) and have trouble finding a single person who does not look back on the Americans' time there as a Golden Age.

BEN FAWCETT

'When the Americans were here,' says one old man who lives in the shanty shacks built on stilts above the Saigon River, 'one person in work could feed a family of eight or nine; now he struggles to feed himself.' It is a common complaint on the streets, and it signals that the rosy memory of the American years has perhaps as much to do with money as with ideology or 'freedom'.

The Americans pumped so much money into South Vietnam that almost everyone benefited. Many people were directly employed as drivers or office workers, and others found work in the entertainment and service industries. Money spent by US soldiers on bar girls would be passed on to the families of those bar girls, and those families bought goods from traders and farmers – everyone finished up better off.

The memory of this comparative affluence means that the Vietnamese Government is judged against impossibly high standards – whatever policy it adopted could not, in the circumstances, have delivered to its people American levels of wealth. But the Party would have had much more chance of pulling people behind a common national purpose if it had not first alienated them by post-Liberation purges that sent thousands to re-education camps and prompted thousands of others to take their chances in boats on the South China Sea.

Left: Hi-tech imports have long been available in the South but Hanoi shops like this one still have the shock of the new.

A half-chance of paradise

One of the things that has harmed Vietnam's image most over the years since reunification has been the exodus of refugees known as 'boat people'. People do not risk their lives in flimsy boats on the typhoon-tossed open seas for nothing; and the assumption has therefore been that they must be running away from something really terrible, from a climate of fear and repression within Vietnam.

For the first wave of 'boat people' which followed the fall of Saigon in 1975 there was some truth in this. People were leaving because they were terrified of what would happen once the Communists were in control; the majority of this first wave were either middle-class people who feared the loss of their businesses, or people with ties to the old regime or service in their army who feared persecution. And those who stayed did indeed see private enterprise frowned upon and thousands of people sent to re-education camps, where they studied Marxism-Leninism and had to express contrition for their past sins before being able to return to normal life. (There is a story in circulation in Vietnam that, after Liberation, the first day people in the South feared for their lives; the second day they feared for their property; the third day they started complaining that there weren't any good programmes on the TV any more!)

But the 'boat people' (many asylum seekers actually travel overland) have continued to leave Vietnam throughout the 1980s, although economic policies have been relaxed and most people have been released from the camps. Why?

Speak to asylum seekers who have recently returned to Hanoi after an unsuccessful attempt to escape through Hong Kong, or to ordinary people in Saigon who are still interested in leaving, and you become convinced that the problem is usually not politics or repression but simply money; they hope for a better life in a rich country. Vietnam has been so impoverished by its decades of war and its ensuing decade and a half of misguided economic policy and isolation from the rest of the global economy that its people are more susceptible to images of wealth elsewhere in the world.

People in Saigon/Ho Chi Minh City and its environs saw rich-world living at first hand when the Americans were in residence, and see no reason why they should now have to live in poverty while others enjoy such plenty. The sense of deprivation is further enhanced by the packages of money and goods which arrive from relatives who have succeeded in settling overseas. In addition, southerners are still treated as 'losers', and many people feel frustrated by subtle but inescapable discrimination which blocks their progress in work and other fields.

Perhaps intentionally, Western policy towards Vietnam has encouraged emigration. This policy is two-fold: there is a 'push' factor, from the impoverishment of the country by the aid and trade embargo imposed by the US after Vietnam invaded Cambodia (President Reagan spoke of 'bleeding Vietnam white' as a punishment); the other factor is the 'pull' of the image of life in

HOWARD DAVIES

In limbo. Up to 1,600 Vietnamese refugees live in each shed of the Shan Shui Po closed camp in Hong Kong. Some of them have been here awaiting resettlement for five years.

the West and the preferential treatment that Vietnamese 'refugees' received. Until 1982, anyone who was able to reach a neighbouring country was almost guaranteed resettlement in a rich Western country, in particular America, Canada, Australia or France. The decades of isolation and poverty have led to a sense of hopelessness amongst most Vietnamese people that things will ever improve.

Over a million Vietnamese are now living as expatriates in Western countries. They form flourishing communities in many cities. Because of the powerful ties of kinship in Vietnamese society, the links remain strong between these overseas Vietnamese, and their families who stayed behind. The money and gifts they send home are a useful contribution to the economy – but also a powerful magnet.

All over the South, there are people who dream of emigrating to the US and solving all their problems at a stroke. For example, amongst a group of poor families living in stilt-houses built out over the Saigon River, all but the two oldest people among them said they would go to the US tomorrow if they had the chance – and they said many of their neighbours in this stilt suburb had left in previous waves of boat people.

Nuong is a 39-year-old woman with two children who tries to keep her family going by temporary work for local farmers out among the paddy fields of the Mekong Delta. The worry of her breadline existence has etched deep lines on her forehead, yet what keeps her going is not the hope of change in her locality or in Vietnam as a whole, but the impossible dream that one day a magic plane ticket to the US (where she has cousins) will rescue her from poverty, undernutrition and insecurity.

Nuong - labourer with an impossible dream.

CHRIS BRAZIER

But people in the North are also not immune to the idea that outside Vietnam the streets are paved with gold. Do Chi Ngoc left Hanoi in July 1988 and bought a passage in a tiny boat at Quang Ninh for about £300 – the whole of his life savings together with part of his mother's. He had, he says, only one reason for leaving.

'Some of my friends had said there was a country that was very rich and like paradise – naturally I wanted to go there. I didn't have any special country in mind... Yes, I felt terrified [of the boat journey] but I was so keen to get to this paradise that I felt it was worth the risk.'

Despite being hit by typhoons on the way, Ngoc eventually reached Hong Kong – but was immediately arrested and housed in a detention centre, where he stayed for almost two years. 'In the end I got the news that none of us would be accepted by a rich country: we'd have to stay in the camps. And I heard the Government in Vietnam would take back anyone who returned voluntarily. But it was the letters from my mother that really made up my mind – she said returned refugees weren't in any trouble.

'Now I work with my little sister on her tea stall. But I'm really just filling in time while I wait for the authorities to allocate me some work – they've promised to let me train in television repair but say I'll have to wait...'

Finding employment is the major problem for people who have returned from Hong Kong. Nguyen Thanh Van, who is a pharmacist by trade, has not applied for her old job in a Hanoi hospital because she is sure that with current unemployment levels she would not be re-employed. Pham Thi Bach Tuyet, on the other hand, will be returning to her former sewing co-operative as soon as she has saved up and bought a sewing machine.

Most of the repatriated asylum seekers have found work in the country's expanding private sector, often selling imported goods in the numerous street markets. Nguyen Thi Than, who was an engineer before he fled, now sells Chinese apples and beer in the streets of Hanoi. 'This is a very different Vietnam from the one I left,' he says. 'Now there are good opportunities for those who want to work hard and have initiative.'

But however much the country has changed, the movement of migrants from poverty will only diminish when the quality of life improves in Vietnam. The international community can help in this by accepting Vietnam back into the fold and removing the trade and aid restrictions which hamper its economic development.

CHRIS BRAZIER

Home from Hong Kong: Do Chi Ngoc.

A people on the move

The Vietnamese traditionally have very close ties to the familiar surroundings of their village and to the land that they inherit from their ancestors. These ties have been strained and broken by the physical destruction caused by warfare, and by the huge movements of population that have taken place over the last forty years.

In 1954, when the country was divided by the Geneva Agreements, more than one million people, most of them Catholic, moved from the North to the South. During the war with the US, eight million people were moved into 'strategic hamlets' by the southern Government, and people migrated from rural areas to the comparative safety of the towns. Large numbers of people in the North were moved from towns and cities which were targets of US bombing. Many spent years living in underground shelters.

Since 1975 about four million people have left the densely populated Delta provinces and central coastal areas, to be resettled in the New Economic Zones in the highlands.

At the end of the war, many of those most closely associated with the previous Thieu regime left South Vietnam, with American assistance. Between 1975 and 1978, about 130,000 arrived in countries of first asylum in SE Asia. Many thousands more lost their lives at sea, as a result of shipwreck, piracy or exposure. By July 1978 about a quarter of a million Vietnamese of Chinese origin had crossed the border into China.

In 1979 the UN High Commissioner for Refugees (UNHCR) convened a conference in Geneva at which some 65 countries pledged resettlement aid and places for 260,000 refugees. Virtually anyone who could reach foreign soil was eligible for resettlement and, in addition, the UNHCR Orderly Departure Programme (ODP), which allowed for emigration to reunite families, was established. Many tens of thousands of people have left Vietnam officially, for Western destinations, under the ODP. During the same period, many more people arrived unofficially in SE Asian countries, by boat, seeking asylum.

In June 1988, with vast numbers of Vietnamese asylum seekers in refugee camps in Hong Kong, a large increase in arrivals, and inadequate resettlement provisions, the Territory's Government introduced screening of people to decide whether they were political refugees, or 'economic migrants' not entitled to resettlement in a host country. Similar screening procedures are now used in other SE Asian countries, and people are increasingly volunteering to be repatriated to Vietnam. The US opposed forced repatriation, and Vietnam was unwilling to give them additional reasons for maintaining the trade embargo; but with a softening of the US attitude on the issue, in October 1991 Vietnam finally acceded to British pressure and agreed to take back even those refugees from the Hong Kong camps who have expressed an unwillingness to go home.

Fate is a card-index. Applications to settle in the rich world from Vietnamese migrants who have landed up in a transit camp in Malaysia.

HOWARD DAVIES

Vietnam's Perestroika: Doi Moi

'Things have been much better in the last five years.' You hear this refrain wherever you go in Vietnam – from the bicycle mechanics to be found on every street corner in Hanoi, offering a speedy puncture repair or service to the streams of people pedalling by; from the young people who have set up stalls selling cigarettes in the streets of provincial towns and villages; from ordinary people who feel much freer to venture their own opinion about things, even to a Westerner.

The five-year time-frame is because momentous changes were set in train at the Sixth Congress of the Vietnamese Communist Party in 1986. The first concessions to market economics had come as long ago as 1979 but it was at the Sixth Congress that *doi moi* or 'new thinking' was approved, and the pragmatic Nguyen Van Linh emerged as General Secretary.

Since then the changes in the everyday life of most Vietnamese have been profound, particularly in the North. Until 1986, private enterprise was frowned upon in Vietnam. In the North, which had been under communist rule since 1954, people were used to a centrally planned economy in which goods were produced and distributed by the State. Western visitors to Hanoi in those years were struck by the strange quietness of its streets – this was largely because the only shops belonged to the State and were usually poorly stocked.

Until 1975, it is fair to say that both the government and the people of North Vietnam were utterly dedicated to winning the war and reuniting the country. People had developed habits of austerity and self-sacrifice from necessity. But once the country was reunified, they had to start thinking about regeneration and development. Vietnam's then leader, Pham Van Dong, admitted frankly: 'Waging a war is simple but running a country is very difficult'. Loss of Chinese support was an important factor in delaying recovery.

By the mid-1980s it had become clear that there was no option but to change direction from the policy of rapid industrialisation. The attempt to collectivise the South had failed miserably, there were food shortages of near-famine proportions, and the economy as a whole was grinding to a halt. As a result the Government launched its ambitious programme of reforms, liberalising the economy to allow private businesses to operate, and actively seeking foreign investment and trade.

In part, *doi moi* echoed the Soviet Union's *perestroika* – but it was launched much more effectively and single-mindedly than Gorbachev's economic reforms of the same period. The Vietnamese rediscovered their own taste and flair for trading and commerce, and thousands of shops, market stalls and small industries sprang up all over the country.

Doi moi has had profound effects in every area of life. In the countryside, land has been leased back to peasant families who now have complete freedom to cultivate their plots and sell their

CHRIS BRAZIER

BEN FAWCETT

Street barbers compete for custom in Hanoi.

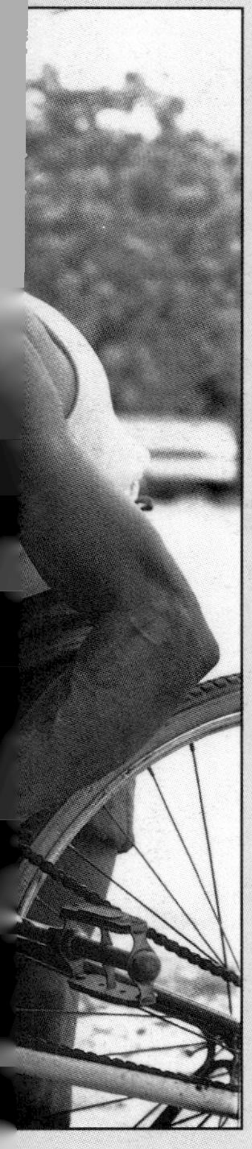

Service with a smile in free-market Hanoi. On every street corner is a bike mechanic ready to offer an overhaul or a puncture repair.

produce. Harvests have markedly increased and, although there are still shortages in certain areas, Vietnam has been transformed from a country chronically short of food to a large-scale exporter of rice. The economy has started to adapt to world market conditions and government economists talk hopefully of Vietnam emulating its thriving capitalist neighbours in East Asia. The climate of repression which operated before 1986, in which people were afraid to speak freely against the government, has now eased.

But there are negative effects, too. Vietnam needed to change, but it was a society which genuinely tried to live up to the ideal of equality. Central planning may have failed to supply people's material needs, but it did mean that people had equal access to a comprehensive system of health care and education. Now the gap between rich and poor is widening and there are few state funds to pay for the public services of which the Vietnamese were once justly proud. The feeling of general equality and collective purpose that once infused the North in particular, is now being fast eroded.

Yet there is no doubt that the *doi moi* reforms are popular – if ordinary people are dissatisfied with them it tends to be because they are impatient with the pace of change rather than because they wish to turn back the clock.

The village tailors in Ron sum things up as well as anybody. Ron lies on the main road just north of the Seventeenth Parallel which once divided the country. Cam and Nhu live in quite a substantial house built with its frontage on the roadside and its back on stilts over the sea. They talk articulately about their lives: Cam travelled as far as Thailand before returning home in 1960 'because my country needed me'; while his wife Nhu has always dreamed of travelling to Europe, 'though I would always want to come home to where my roots are'.

'We feel a lot better off as a result of *doi moi*,' says Cam. 'If you looked at this village and actually weighed up how much more or less people earned you might say the changes had been small – and that some people have actually ended up poorer. But we just feel it's a better, more sensible way of operating.'

Back to the family farm

In the Vietnamese countryside, burdens are carried by means of a long pole across the shoulders with a load at either end. The peasants of Nghe Tinh, historically Vietnam's poorest province, see themselves and their narrow strip of land as bearing the burden of the two great river Deltas at either end of the country.

The image of Vietnam as a peasant's shoulder pole drives home the fact that this is a predominantly agricultural nation – over 70 per cent of Vietnamese people earn their living from the soil. And their lives, too, have changed dramatically under *doi moi*. After 1954 the Government of North Vietnam introduced major land reform and grouped peasants into co-operatives which managed the land and distributed food and welfare services on the basis of need. And when Hanoi gained control of the South, including the vast and fertile Mekong Delta, it tried to extend this collectivisation of agriculture.

The attempt was a failure and rice production per person plummeted in the southern provinces – by 1986 it was lower than it had been in 1942. The Government concentrated on developing an industrial base, and there was virtually no investment in agriculture. Prices paid to farming communes had been set low so as to provide cheap food for industrial workers, which left peasants with little incentive. Throughout rural Vietnam a system designed to guarantee basic needs was failing to deliver. The average amount of calories available per person was so close to subsistence that substantial numbers of people must have been undernourished. To tackle these problems, in 1981 the Vietnamese Government replaced the co-operative workpoint system with a 'contract' system which allowed them to keep what they produced over and above a certain quota. This had little effect; and by 1987 there were severe food shortages.

In 1988 the *doi moi* policy was applied to agriculture. Food prices were raised to realistic market levels. And, under Resolution 10, farmers were given long-term tenure of their land on a 15-year lease. State subsidies on food rations and farm supplies were abolished. This effectively ended the collective system – peasants now sell their own produce on the free market, where private traders compete with the state procurement companies. Apart from paying the government agricultural tax, which is based on the fertility of the land and in most cases averages around 10 per cent of their output, farmers can dispose of their income however they wish – though they must buy the fertilisers, pesticides and seeds which the co-operative once provided, and pay a tax to the co-operative for services.

The results were immediate and spectacular. After many years of having to import food, and a severe food shortage in 1988, Vietnam exported 1.4 million tonnes of rice in 1989,

KEITH BERNSTEIN

Farming is very much a family affair in Vietnam. Every handful of rice threshed now contributes to the family income.

Wet rice cultivation, using buffalo for ploughing.

Food production in Vietnam since reunification

The following figures show annual per capita production in kilograms of paddy (rice with husk) equivalent:

Year	Rice	Other cereals
1976	241	34
1980	217	51
1985	265	39
1986	262	39
1987	242	39
1988	267	41
1989	293	39
1990	289	36

KEITH BERNSTEIN

making it the third largest rice exporter in the world that year, behind Thailand and the US. Social scientists at Hanoi's Institute of Economics found that productivity had doubled from 3-4 tonnes to 7-8 tonnes per hectare per year in some places.

This rapid increase in food production has probably done more to rally people behind *doi moi* than any other single development. Take Huu Tho, who as deputy editor of the Communist Party's daily newspaper, *Nhan Dan*, must have been responsible over the years for a great deal of propaganda about the value of the collective system. 'The meaning of socialism has also changed for me,' he said. 'We always used to have a rice shortage every year. But now that we have changed the system and allowed people to produce for themselves we not only have enough to eat but also enough for export as well. I am persuaded that this is the right way for our country to advance from extreme poverty.' There is always a danger, though, that too much emphasis on exports will obscure the fact that some areas still run short of basic foods. Vietnam remains a very poor country.

Party functionaries have to be behind the reforms if they are to continue in office. But the best judges of the changes in agriculture are clearly the farmers themselves. Mai Thi Bic lives in the hills of northern Bac Thai province. Here the land is much less fertile than in the Red River Delta, with its rich alluvial soils stretching south to Hanoi and beyond. On each hectare of cultivable land, several families struggle to make a living. Bic's parents moved to the area more than half a century ago because of the starvation in their home village but their new home hardly proved to be a land of milk and honey. A widow of 66, who lost two sons in the war against the Americans, Bic has had the hardest of lives. Yet she feels she has at last lived to see better times.

'Things have been very different in the last few years – we now have our own land to work. And the wind makes my face cool – which is our way of saying things are much better. Before 1986 it was rather difficult, not just for me but for all farmers. Now we work the land when it is necessary, whereas in the old days we had to go out to the fields every day or else we'd lose our communal provision. To speak frankly – in those days we didn't have enough food and sometimes had nothing but soup to eat. Now there is more food. It's still not as much as we'd like because here the population is big and the land is small. But at least now we can manage.'

At the other end of the country, in the Mekong Delta province of Long An, Tuan is of a similar age to Bic but is a very different kind of farmer. In the South the collapse of collectivisation meant that land reverted to its previous owners, which meant that Tuan regained the two hectares of land he bought way back in 1963 with money he'd saved from work in fishing. The reforms have pushed up his standard of living to a level Bic could only dream of. Whereas Bic says if she had more money she would simply buy more food, Tuan has already equipped his house with a television set, a video and a cassette deck.

But the more important contrast is between Tuan and the people in his own neighbourhood, whom he employs to work in his fields on a casual basis. These poorer people, whom collectivisation was designed to benefit, have been left high and dry by the reforms. They have no land of their own and must rely on finding employment with those that do have it – often there is not enough work to go round.

It reminds us of the peasants' image of the shoulder pole, which showed that, even under a communist system, there were great inequalities between regions due to differences in soil fertility, and population pressures. *Doi moi* has already started to deliver the agricultural goods – but some people are bound to benefit from it more than others.

Tuan, proud to point to his own two hectares of earth.

The farmer in the shadow of the Dam

Le Sy Chinh lives in the shadow of the Dong Be Dam, built with Oxfam support, in Trieu Son district. His family have lived in this area since 1962, and he moved back here in 1985 when he left the army.

'I was born here, and grew up here; but our house was in the middle of the proposed reservoir so we had to move, just a few hundred metres. When we heard about the Dam, we had a meeting of the families involved to decide where to move to, whether to move only a short distance away or out of the district altogether.

'That was when we decided to move only a little distance from our original homes. At the beginning I felt very sad to leave my old home, but now we are very happy.'

His parents live just 200 metres away. He has seven brothers and sisters, all of whom live nearby. His eldest sister is 50 and lives only a matter of metres away, his second brother works in the district hospital, and his third brother is a soldier who has just left the forces. All the brothers served in the army.

Chinh, who left the army four years ago, fought in Cambodia where he contracted malaria. For the first two months after he returned from the army he had a bad bout of malaria, but after treatment he now only suffers intermittent attacks; 'whenever I work hard and feel tired'.

'When I returned to this village and my parents' home,' says Chinh, 'the co-operative supplied me with 90 kilos of rice – 45 free and a further 45 at half price – so that I could look for work here or in other areas, and to see if I could go back to agricultural work. After such a long time in the army, I might not have been able to handle it. The rice rations meant that I was not a burden on my

Dong Be Dam.
The reservoir is beginning to fill up; the spillway is still under construction (right foreground).

Up in the mountains, this Hmong farmer is making the most of the breeze to winnow his newly-harvested rice crop.

BEN FAWCETT

parents. Gradually I got used to working in the fields again and relearnt my old skills, and went back to full-time agricultural work. Then I settled down and married.'

Chinh thinks that in general it is difficult to readjust to civilian life after the army. It is often even harder to find a bride. 'But for me it was very easy,' he explains , 'as I was introduced to my wife by her older sister, who was in the army with me, after we returned.'

The construction of the dam has helped improve people's standard of living. The rice output has more than doubled because of the increased access to water. 'Besides rice, I grow sweet potatoes, bananas and other kinds of fruit trees,' says Chinh, 'because the increased water supply for irrigation means the soil is moist enough for fruit production. The trees look much greener now and bear far more fruit. In the past we would have liked to grow jackfruit, guavas and apples but there was not enough water – now we can also grow many more vegetables, for our animals and for ourselves.'

To make the most of the land's increased potential, Chinh and the other farmers need to use new seed varieties and fertilisers, although they do use organic fertilisers. 'Everything, new seed varieties, fertilisers and pesticides, used to come from the co-operative through their investment scheme, but now under the contract system we have to buy everything, at the fixed state price. We're prepared to buy these things as they increase our harvests.

'In the past, there was a lack of incentives. The lazy and the hard workers got the same, which was very discouraging for hard-working people. Now it all depends on the family; the more they work, the more they earn – it's all up to them.'

KEITH BERNSTEIN

KEITH BERNSTEIN

***Above:** The tranquil beauty of water, sky and rice fields, central Vietnam. The fields in the background have been flooded in preparation for planting out rice seedlings.*

***Left:** Since the* doi moi *changes, people are able to sell their own produce in street markets. Vietnamese farmers grow a very wide range of fruit and vegetables.*

SARAH LOCK

BEN FAWCETT

Above: Madonnas, pop stars and communist flags go to make up a rich cultural mix on the streets of Hanoi. The flags are celebrating the 45th Anniversary of Independence.

BEN FAWCETT

Right: Buddhist deity, on guard at the entrance to a historic pagoda, beside the Perfume River on the outskirts of Hué.

Left: A mural for the 100th Anniversary of Ho Chi Minh's birth.

SARAH LOCK

Right: In the South, people are eager for the consumer goods which go with a Western life-style. The motorbikes are mostly Japanese imports.

A long and rocky road

A tiny roadside stall, just big enough for the proprietor to sit in behind the display of locally made beer and soft drinks, sweets, instant noodles, and packs of Hero cigarettes. It could be anywhere in Vietnam, though in the cities you might expect to find Dunhill and 555 cigarettes alongside the Vietnamese-made ones (which are considered vastly inferior).

But this stall is in a tiny village just south of Dong Hoi in central Vietnam: it stands on the corner where the one-storey houses give way to the paddy fields, and it is run by Hoa. She's 20 years old though, like most Vietnamese, she looks quite a bit younger to the Western eye. She only started this stall four months ago when she finished school, and still has to do her share of work in the family's fields, but already she is earning the equivalent of about £2.50 a day by buying goods in the town and then selling them here at a 20 per cent mark-up. Hers is the kind of entrepreneurial initiative which would have been frowned upon in Vietnam only five years ago, yet the change has been so complete that Hoa has little sense of how different things were in the past – and she dismisses the war against the US with an abrupt 'Who wants to talk about that!'

Just as Hoa's is an utterly typical roadside stall, so she could stand as a symbol of Vietnam's economy as it flutters into life: brash, forward-looking and full of initiative but as yet operating on a very small scale.

Even in the ever-diminishing state sector, small co-operatives and bigger factories express the new spirit of enterprise. Factory managers are beginning to talk like their capitalist counterparts. 'Growth is the only solution,' says the manager of the Dong Tam Engineering Company on the outskirts of Ho Chi Minh City, 'and we must produce what the people want.'

Ingenuity is being encouraged. 'We can copy everything, but we lack money,' says the young manager of a newly-started family business in Ho Chi Minh City. 'Last year we copied a Japanese rice mill, and now we produce a stone-cutting machine copied from an Italian catalogue mailed to us by a member of our family living in Europe.'

And everyone, from the street sellers to the policy makers, seems optimistic that Vietnam can launch itself down the capitalist road with great success. But for the moment that process is still hampered by the embargo on Western trade and official aid that was imposed at the time of Vietnam's invasion of Cambodia, in 1979.

Vietnam's economy has in recent years relied heavily on aid from and trade with the Soviet Union and Eastern Europe. Since 1978, when Vietnam joined the CMEA, the socialist bloc's common market, it has received well over a billion dollars worth of aid every year from those countries. Much of this has been concentrated in large and important infrastructure projects, such as electricity generation at the massive Hoa Binh hydro-power dam. A large trade deficit has also built up between Vietnam and CMEA countries. Since the major political changes that have taken place in Eastern Europe, this economic and political support is no longer

CHRIS BRAZIER

Hoa and her typical roadside stall, one of thousands that have opened since the economy was liberalised.

CHRIS BRAZIER

Up to the minute electronics, timeless transport. Just about every street in Hanoi now seems to have a shop piled to the ceiling with boxes of the latest Japanese videos and stereos.

forthcoming, and Russia is demanding repayments of its loans to Vietnam, in dollars rather than roubles. As a result, Vietnam is now desperate to open its doors and arms to all comers. The Government has introduced the most liberal foreign-investment laws in South-East Asia, but hitherto only its East Asian neighbours have really taken advantage. Trade with Japan, Singapore and South Korea is beginning to take off, and Taiwanese entrepreneurs in particular have begun investing in businesses in Ho Chi Minh City, convinced that Vietnam represents the region's most lucrative investment in the long term. Taiwan is now the biggest foreign investor in Vietnam, responsible for $439 million worth of projects up to June 1991.

Vietnam, after all, is a country rich in natural resources – and with the thirteenth highest population in the world it has a large domestic market waiting to be tapped if living standards start to take off. The hope is that if Western companies see sufficient potential advantage they will disregard the political implications; although the economic policy of the US remains a powerful influence. US companies have themselves been engaging in behind the scenes lobbying to get the embargo lifted, recognising the opportunities they are missing. Vietnam has concluded deals with oil companies from nine countries, with Britain most heavily involved, by which they will share the profits from any oil or gas which is found on a 50-50 basis. The US company Mobil, banned from direct trading relationships with Vietnam, has been seeking a way into these oilfields by the back door – a 'joint venture' with the Russians.

A review of Vietnam by an international investment firm stated that the long-term potential of the country was impressive: 'proven oil reserves are amongst the largest in the world, but years of exploration will be needed to bring them into use'.

Oil may help, but oil alone is certainly not going to work an economic miracle. Even if the international barriers come down, Vietnam is going to have great trouble adjusting to the rigours of the global market. The fact that average factory wages in Vietnam are lower than in any other Asian country (except Bangladesh) may help it to find overseas markets, in the early stages, for its light industrial products, such as clothing and footwear. But the Vietnamese legal and banking structures need to be brought into line with international standards before investors will have real confidence in the economy. The apparent ambition of government economists to emulate the success of the 'Four Little Tigers' – Taiwan, South Korea, Singapore and Hong Kong – seems more than a little fanciful at the moment.

The road that runs past Hoa's stall is rutted and pitted. It is Vietnam's main arterial highway, and its state of disrepair illustrates the difficulties that Vietnam has had in renewing its infrastructure after the devastation of the war – and that in turn is a major obstacle in the way of economic progress. Whether Hoa looks to the north or the south, the road ahead of her, and the nascent market economy she symbolises, is long and decidedly rocky.

The doctor is out selling...

'The health system here is good but there is no content to it. You see what I mean? The Vietnamese health system is a model for the way it goes from the centre to the province to the district to the commune. Perfect! But the content! There's no medicine, no equipment and no personnel. The medical personnel aren't working, they're busy selling things in the street to make a living.' So says Dr Duong Quynh Hoa, who should know since she was Minister of Health between 1975 and 1976 and has since been Director of the Children's Hospital in Ho Chi Minh City.

The problem she refers to is a recent one and is a worrying downside of the *doi moi* reforms. Communist Vietnam had a health strategy which was a shining example for a country in its position. All too many developing countries have followed a Western model of health care, building expensive, prestige hospitals in the towns but neglecting the needs of ordinary rural people for simple but sometimes life-saving treatment, and preventive medicine. In contrast, long before the international community started promoting the concept, one of Vietnam's strengths as a society was its investment in primary health care – every village had its own clinic, staffed by people with medical training that was limited but enabled them to deal with certain common illnesses and health needs. More complicated cases were referred on to polyclinics or hospitals elsewhere in the district or province. Meanwhile, the clinic staff could also concentrate on community health education programmes – on topics such as malaria, nutrition and birth control.

But this health-care system was part and parcel of a collectivised economic and social system – the funds to pay the clinic staff and buy medicines and equipment came out of collective surpluses generated in agriculture or industry. Now that the economy has been substantially privatised, there are no longer the funds available to support such a health network.

The result is that the principle of free health care has been undermined. Local clinics still offer free care, though it is a lucky patient who finds medical staff available or the appropriate medicines in the cupboard. Consultation fees have now been introduced at hospitals. Treatment fees are extra: as examples, an appendectomy costs around £6 and delivery of a baby £2. In theory the poor are still supposed to be exempt from fees if they produce a certificate from their local authority. But in one district hospital surveyed, the number of inpatients fell by 50 per cent when fees were introduced.

This is likely to have a significant effect on general levels of public health, unless people's incomes rise much faster than looks likely at the moment. In the long term, once-prevalent diseases which have been virtually eliminated, such as typhoid, tuberculosis and leprosy, might return. And in the short term, the dysentery and diarrhoea which are rife in Vietnam are likely to take their toll – these conditions are the world's main killers of children, but prove the value of primary health care in that they can be simply and effectively treated by even an under-resourced local clinic. If people

CHRIS BRAZIER

KEITH BERNSTEIN

Left: Dr Duong Quynh Hoa.

Help at hand in a rural clinic – but patients now will probably have to pay for treatment.

have to go further and start paying for health care, more children will inevitably slip through the net.

The crisis in health funding will make an effective response to Vietnam's current malaria epidemic very difficult (see below). Family planning, which currently is given high priority, is also likely to suffer. The shortage of funds is openly admitted at every level. Dr Vo Thi Kim Anh says that nowadays doctors are commonly compared to farm animals 'because they have to work very hard but receive nothing in return'. Her own salary of 40,000 dong (£3) a month bears this out: she is Director of one of Danang's three main hospitals, yet she earns a fraction of what an ordinary urban Vietnamese considers to be a decent living wage, and little more than half what her husband does as a labourer on the railways. 'All equipment and medicine in the hospital used to be paid for by the Government,' she says. 'Now we receive about two million dong a month – enough to cover salaries plus electricity and

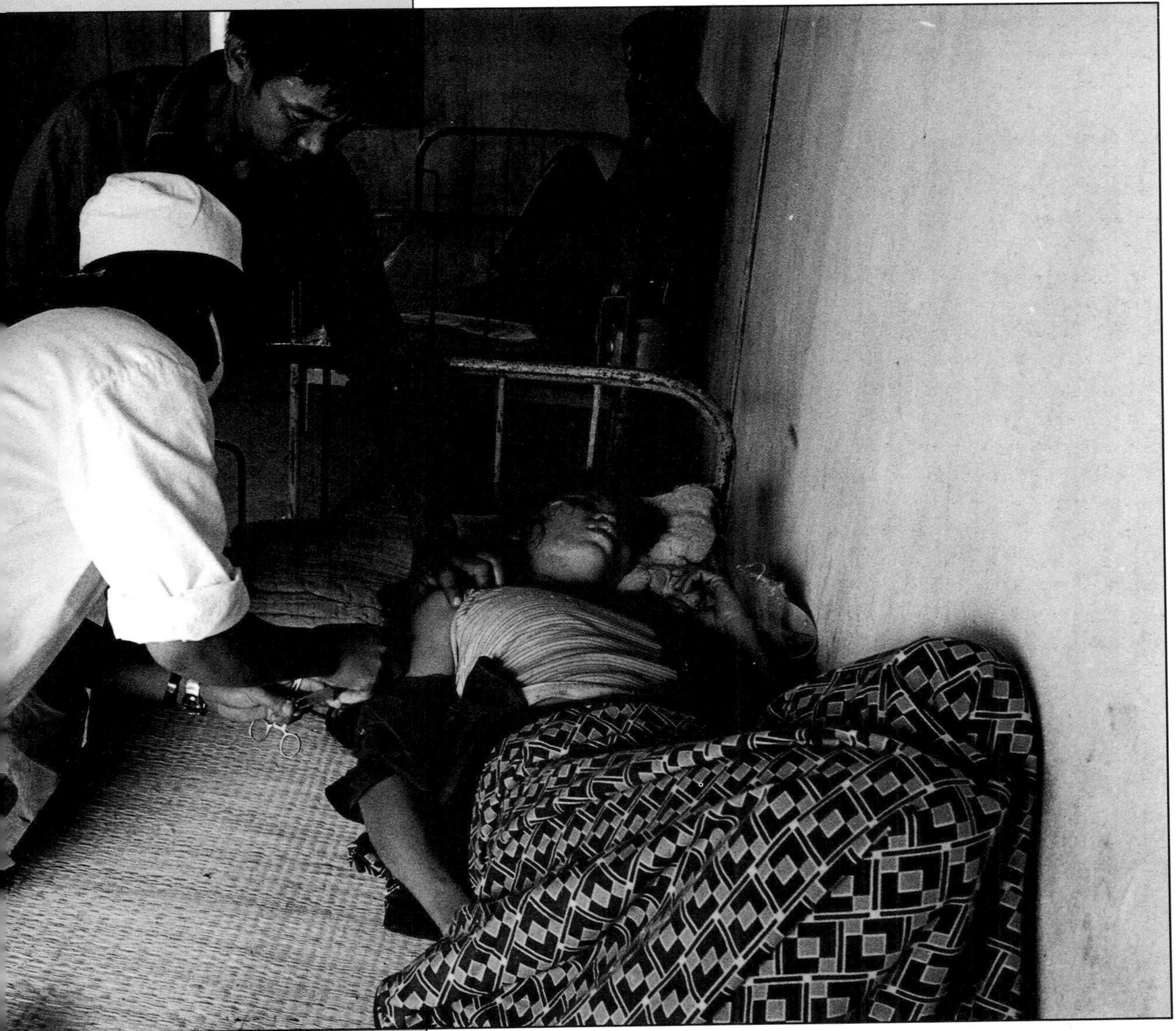

water costs. But it won't buy us any equipment and patients must pay for some treatment now.' In 1990 a Western charity paid for her to visit Thailand and she was impressed by the Thai health system. 'We could learn some things from Thailand but others would be difficult to apply in Vietnam. In Thailand they use good equipment to treat patients. In Vietnam the equipment is poor, but the doctors have a kindness, humanity and enthusiasm which makes up some of the shortfall – in this respect, at least, we are equal.'

Watch out, there's a mosquito about! A poster from the anti-malarial campaign.

Birth control

A group of women from a Women's Union branch in Ky Anh district were surprisingly well-informed about methods of contraception; they had heard of the diaphragm, sterilisation, the Pill, the rhythm method, and a new drug called quinacrine. Unfortunately, apart from the rhythm method, none of these methods were available to them, either at the health centre for their commune, or the district centre. All of them had at one time or another been fitted with an intra-uterine device (IUD), a large plastic type without a thread, copied from a Czechoslovakian model, which is the only form of contraception available in Vietnam. But many of the women had the device removed because they experienced pain and bleeding, and had lost weight. The result was that almost all of them had undergone at least one abortion; some had had as many as four.

That this picture is typical of the rest of Vietnam is borne out by statistics: 89 per cent of those using modern methods of contraception use the IUD. Male methods, such as condoms or vasectomy, are hardly used at all, and birth control is considered a women's problem and responsibility. One in three pregnancies in Vietnam ends in abortion – which means about one million abortions a year. Women want quite small families (the average desired family size is 2.6 children), which is not surprising in a country where people marry relatively late, in their mid-twenties, and where the majority of women are literate, and most work outside the household. A better family planning service is urgently needed, with health personnel who have more time for each client, are better trained and can offer a greater choice of methods, for men as well as women.

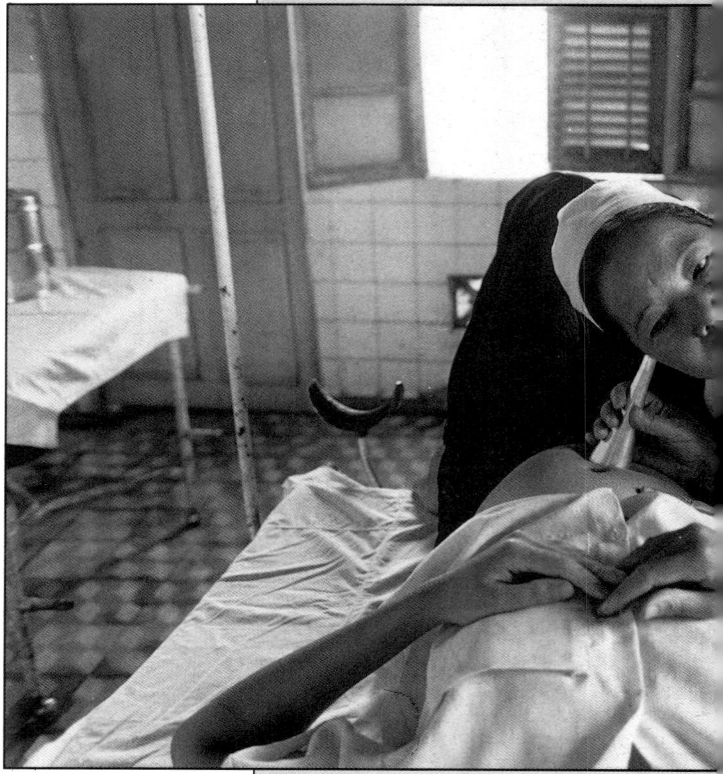

KEITH BERNSTEIN

This foetal heart beats good and strong – but one in three pregnancies in Vietnam ends in abortion.

The new battle: malaria

Vietnam is facing a major malaria epidemic and there are fears that the incidence of the disease will rise even further unless the government is able to extend its anti-malarial campaign. To do that will require a massive injection of foreign aid.

BEN FAWCETT

Malaria in South-East Asia is generally on the increase. According to Dr Do Duc Thuy, the Director of the Malaria Institute in Hanoi, some 15 per cent of Vietnamese people suffer from malaria. In some of the worst affected areas, such as the mountainous and border regions, malaria has incapacitated 25 per cent of the population, and medical experts are worried that the incidence of malaria in Vietnam could rise to affect nearly half the population.

Malaria is transmitted by mosquitoes which have sucked up the malaria parasite during a previous blood meal from an infected person. One of the reasons for the recent dramatic increase in malaria cases may be the half a million soldiers returned from Cambodia, many of whom are infected. The situation is aggravated by the fact that the parasites, especially the falciparum species which is responsible for the deadly cerebral form of malaria, have become resistant to common and cheap anti-malarial drugs, such as chloroquine. Mosquitoes have also developed resistance to some insecticides.

The Malaria Institute is developing new methods to combat malaria. One of its most recent experiments is impregnating mosquito nets with an insecticide called permethrin, an effective deterrent against mosquitoes. These nets could help to reduce the transmission of malaria, but in some areas local people do not like using them. So, instead, curtains have been impregnated with permethrin and people have been encouraged to hang these up in their homes to try to reduce mosquito numbers. 'Initial results show a drastic reduction of up to 60-70 per cent in malaria cases over the six months' trial period,' says Dr Thuy. To remain effective, the nets must be reimpregnated every few months. The use of nets is only part of the elimination strategy. Icon sprays, replacing the use of DDT, can be used to treat the interior walls of houses. This effectively kills any mosquitoes which come in contact with the treated walls. Unfortunately, such new and effective insecticides are expensive and have to be imported, and Vietnam does not have the foreign exchange to pay for them.

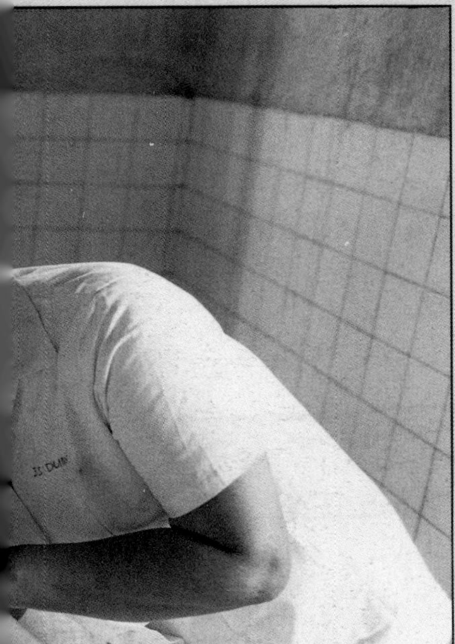

There are just not enough resources within Vietnam to invest in full-scale preventative and eradication programmes. 'We have no preventive drugs for malaria,' says Dr Thuy. 'We need the help of international organisations for the next few years if we are to reduce the incidence of malaria. At present all we can do is to try to contain the current epidemic.'

A most literate nation

The school has been half-demolished by the typhoon winds. The roof has been whipped away and half the walls are now nothing but rubble spilling on to the wet earth. In a classroom that is still standing, the last lesson before the storm is still chalked up on the blackboard.

The District Chairperson, Mr Din, looks doleful, as well he might. A teacher by profession himself, as are other members of his family, education is much more to him than just another local-government responsibility. He knows that the community school is as good a symbol as any of what Vietnam has managed to give its people since it won independence after the Second World War.

Learning has always been important in Vietnam – its first national university was founded as long ago as 1076 (around the same time as Oxford University in England) and it has a long and rich literary tradition. But under the emperors it was the exclusive province of a tiny elite and remained so throughout the French colonial period: by 1945 around 90 per cent of the population was still illiterate.

Nationalists like Ho Chi Minh always saw education – and particularly literacy – as a vital factor in their campaign. The more people understood, the less resigned they would be to their own exploitation. This is why they were so keen to support the writing of Vietnamese in the Latinised *quoc ngu* script – it made mass literacy much more possible.

Education remained a top priority once they were in government, and Vietnam's educational successes have been remarkable, given the country's limited resources. The adult literacy rate remains high, at 82 per cent. The number of girls attending primary school is very nearly equal to the number of boys, in sharp contrast to many other developing countries. And almost all children have for decades been guaranteed access to the first five years of school.

The investment in basic education for all was one of the cornerstones of the communist system. The trouble is that over the last decade, as that system has started to fragment, state education has started to fragment too. Whereas in 1980 about 96 per cent of children attended primary school, by 1985 only 86 per cent did so. The proportion now is probably closer to two-thirds and an increasing number of children are leaving without completing their primary schooling.

This is all part and parcel of the changes in the Vietnamese economy. As the communal system breaks down, families are having to make their living in a competitive market. Whereas

KEITH BERNSTEIN

Vietnam has a good record for equality of opportunity in education, and literacy rates for men and women are almost the same.

KEITH BERNSTEIN

The Vietnamese are keen learners but the school system is under threat from lack of resources.

once they lost nothing by sending their child to school, now they often need an extra pair of hands in the rice fields or on the roadside drinks stall. Under *doi moi,* the economic pressure is intense.

Take Tran My Hanh, an eight-year-old girl who sells cigarettes by the road near Cu Chi. 'This is my mother's stall,' she explains, 'and I usually just work here after school or in the holidays. But now my mother is ill, so I've taken over the stall – I am the eldest and can read a bit already, and I'm good at counting.' She puts up the stall at six every morning and works right through to nightfall at seven. She says she's glad she can help the family, though her great ambition is to train as a doctor – she doesn't know if she will ever go back to school.

The market has found its way inside the schools, too. The state no longer has the funds to support free universal education. Until 1989 the first 12 years of schooling were free; now only the first three years are. After that the fee is between 15 and 40 cents a month (tied to the price of rice) and textbooks are sold wherever possible. In addition, teachers have been allowed to set up private classes. Inflation had eaten into their salaries and morale was low; many had ceased to take their jobs seriously and were putting more energy into making money through petty commerce. At least now their money-making activity might still be educational.

One of the saddest aspects of the current changes in Vietnam is that an education system of which it could be justly proud has begun to unravel. The country could yet pay the price for this in the long term. It is already acutely short of the highly trained graduates it needs if it is to find its way in a sophisticated global marketplace. The erosion of basic education could leave it even more disadvantaged.

The 1980s have seen the economic wind rip into the school system. The big question now is the same as the one that faced the District Chairperson after the typhoon: where will the funds come from to rebuild it?

CHRIS BRAZIER

Nowadays, children like this girl from Hué take time out of school to boost the family income.

Women are equal to men ... but

Wherever you go in rural Vietnam, you are received by men. You will sit drinking tea and trading courtesies with the local dignitaries – usually members of the village People's Committee. Ask how many female members there are of the Committee, and of the 14 or 15 there will seldom be more than one woman and often none. And meanwhile women will flit in and out, topping up the teapot, or seeing to the meal.

It is the same the world over, of course, but Vietnam is unlike most other countries in having enshrined women's rights at the core of its constitution. Women are not only proclaimed to be equal to men but two laws specifically demand that men take account of this: the Marriage and Family Law of 1959 ruled that sons and daughters must be treated equally and that the husband must help with child rearing; and a 1986 Act stated that child care and household chores are the joint responsibility of husband and wife.

But these laws have so far had little effect. Of course, some men are prepared to help with household chores and take a share in looking after their children, but domestic work and child rearing remains primarily the responsibility of women. The vast majority of women (97 per cent of women in the countryside, according to the 1989 Census) also engage in economic activities, whether in agriculture or commerce. According to recent research by two Vietnamese sociologists, rural women spend nearly 18 hours a day working compared with men's 14 hours.

This disproportionate burden has increased significantly since the liberalisation of the economy, both because of the extra opportunities to boost the household's cash income and because the old health, education and nursery services have been eroded.

It is this workload which partly explains women's absence from political life. Of the 44 provincial heads of People's Committees only one is a woman; while the proportion of women in Vietnam's National Assembly has sunk from one-third 20 years ago to just 17 per cent now. During the war women were far more involved in public life than they are today.

'To be quite candid,' says Nguyen Thi Binh, one of the few women in a senior government position, 'women work too hard to have time to get involved in political work. The country's poverty has prevented women from enjoying equal rights.'

The official rhetoric has at least had one effect – even women from the remotest rural areas of

BEN FAWCETT

BEN FAWCETT

Learning to operate wood-working machinery in a furniture workshop. Women in Vietnam have a wide range of jobs open to them.
A Women's Union Committee in Nghe Tinh meeting to discuss a pig-breeding scheme.

Vietnam will state that they are the equals of men. Often, though, they will follow that statement by showing that they also believe housework and child care to be the province of women.

Take Truc, a 36-year-old guard at a level crossing on the national railway in Pho Khanh province. In her smart uniform and responsible position she looks the very image of a woman with equal status, and she says 'I think women are equal to men – more and more now'. But she continues: 'Of course women have to do more. I have to do all the things around the house. But that's women's work. It would be possible for men and women to swap roles – for example, my husband does everything when I'm ill. But I wouldn't say that was desirable.'

Or consider Doctor Vo Thi Kim Anh, in her extremely responsible position as Director of one of Danang's three main hospitals. She has three children of between 4 and 14 years old, and once work at the hospital has finished she has to dedicate herself to looking after them and the house – she shops in the market, makes dinner, does the washing and cleaning until eleven at night and is up again at five. At 39 she says 'I feel old because I am always so busy. Yet because of my career I am very happy – I feel I work hard and I work well.'

She seems to feel no resentment at her extra burden, saying, 'I think Vietnamese women are equal enough with men. Woman's work is the Vietnamese way. It's the traditional style of Vietnam. Vietnamese women have femininity. Japan is a very developed country yet when a Japanese woman's husband comes home she takes off his shoes and makes a meal for him. This is also a tradition in Vietnam.' She bridles a bit at the feminist tilt to the questioning yet concludes with a smiling: 'As you know, Vietnamese women can bear anything – we have no alternative'.

The ideas of modern Western feminism have made little inroad in Vietnam. The main women's organisation, the Vietnam Women's Union, has nationwide respect and an impressive total of 11 million members. Yet its activities tend to foster women's traditional role in society – it runs sewing and embroidery classes for girls, and encourages women to be 'good wives and mothers'.

Dr Duong Quynh Hoa, one of Vietnam's most prominent women and an outspoken critic of the Government, is also trenchant in her assessment of the state of Vietnamese women. 'For me the liberation of women in Vietnam is just hot air. Which is to say that the liberation of women means giving women a lot of work, loading them with responsibilities without giving them any rights.'

The image of equality – railway worker, Truc.

CHRIS BRAZIER

Battered by nature

'Vietnam has always been plagued by natural disasters,' says Nguyen Ngoc Dong, Director of the Flood and Storm Control Commission. Situated on the edge of the storm basin of the Pacific Ocean, the long coastline of Vietnam is constantly battered by typhoons.

Vietnamese count themselves lucky if they only have to suffer five to ten major typhoons in any one year – 1989 was particularly bad with 30 severe storms. The first hit in May and the last in October. According to the official statistics, 484 people died and a further 2,004 were injured. A quarter of a million homes were washed away, and two million others suffered extensive flood damage or lost their roofs; 2,000 clinic buildings were completely destroyed and a further 3,500 were badly damaged; 10,000 classrooms collapsed and another 33,000 were damaged.

Nearly a quarter of a million hectares of rice paddy were destroyed, and a further half a million hectares badly affected. In addition, many hectares of other crops, vegetables and fruit were lost. Vietnam's limited economic infrastructure also took a beating with millions of cubic metres of earth washed from dykes and sea defences, miles of roads destroyed, and electricity cables and poles washed away.

This sort of damage is sustained in Vietnam nearly every year. No sooner have the people in the high-risk areas managed to rebuild their homes and replant their crops, than they have to prepare for the next year's onslaught. There is often also extensive seawater flooding, which leaves the flat, coastal land infertile because of the increased salinity levels.

Frequent river floods also cause considerable loss and damage. Although moderate flooding is an annual event in many parts of the country, when heavy rains cause the major rivers to flood, for example, the Red River in 1945 and 1971, the Perfume River in 1975 and the Mekong River in 1961, 1966, 1978 and 1984, flood damage and loss of life reach disaster levels. The Ministry of Water Resources, of which the Flood and Storm Commission is part, has been developing programmes for minimising the damage caused by floods. They have encouraged and overseen the building of dykes on rivers and by the sea, the building of dams and reservoirs, and organised tree planting upstream to control soil erosion and water run-off. The Ministry has also encouraged the development of crop strains which might fare better in areas that are

BEN FAWCETT

Floods wash over Highway Number One as Typhoon Becky takes its toll in Ky Anh.

***Eye on the storm.* Outside the glassless window of the corrugated-iron house in Hué, the typhoon rages on.**

CHRIS BRAZIER

frequently subject to flooding. The use of short-term rice paddy, to avoid the flood season, has proved very successful in the Mekong Delta area.

The Commission is aware of the importance of education and public information as part of flood awareness. They have been developing an early-warning system, to enable the rapid evacuation which will save lives. But much of the country's flood-control measures are actually implemented at the local government level.

Typhoons will continue to plague Vietnam's long coastline but with international aid and the immense efforts of local people, much can be done to reduce the devastation.

Typhoon Becky hits Ky Anh

Every year the area around Ky Anh in central Vietnam suffers devastating damage from natural disasters. 'In recent years,' says Nguyen Din, Chair of the district's People's Committee, 'Ky Anh has had to cope with continual natural calamities which cause heavy loss of life, crops and livestock.' In 1989 the region was hit by three separate typhoons in October alone.

Part of Oxfam's work in Ky Anh has been to support the repair of the district's 63 kilometres of sea dykes damaged by typhoons, and the building of a new dyke, started in 1989. In late August 1990, two of Oxfam's field team from Hanoi, in Ky Anh on a routine monitoring trip, were caught in the year's first tropical storm, Typhoon Becky.

All day Tuesday, 28 August, the local radio broadcast storm warnings as Typhoon Becky drifted towards the Vietnamese coast. It soon became apparent that the storm was heading directly for Ky Anh. After hearing the storm warnings, everyone tried to reinforce their roofs with bamboo or straw and buttressed their walls as best they could. Windows and doors were firmly secured. Fishing boats out at sea, hearing the storm warnings on Vietnamese radio, returned to shore in good time. Patients in the district hospital were moved to the more secure ground-floor rooms in the new typhoon-proof building, and patients in the polyclinics were sent home for safety.

On Tuesday night, around 8 pm, the rain started and the wind began to increase in speed and strength. All this was constantly monitored by the district's meteorological station just outside Ky Anh town. The wind grew in ferocity throughout the night and into the next morning. Windspeed increased in the afternoon, averaging around 180 km per hour and peaking at 7 pm with speeds of up to 194 km per hour. The furious winds turned in an easterly direction and whipped up the sea. Huge waves crashed into shore. High tide coincided with the highest wind speeds.

During the typhoon the district leaders set up a crisis centre in the district town hall, and tried to keep a running account of the damage. There was a string of messengers from every commune passing through the headquarters, reporting the extent of storm damage in their locality. Telephone communications were down during the storm, so everything had to be done in person. Local officials visited every house in their area, finding out the extent of the destruction. Throughout the storm the district officials tried continually to reach areas that were at particular risk, by jeep, motorbike, bicycle, or on foot, so as to advise and assist those in need.

The next day, after the storm, everyone was up early and beginning to tackle the repairs. By 8 am thousands of people were out on their roofs replacing tiles and thatch; furniture and clothing had been dragged outside into the morning sun to dry. People whose houses had suffered extensive damage were piling up bricks and erecting temporary shelters in which to live while they rebuilt their homes. Roadside traders were patching up their thatched stalls ready to resume business.

The most serious damage done by the typhoon was not to people's houses but to the rice fields. The wind whipped up the level of the sea to the point where it overwhelmed the long dyke protecting the paddy fields which was in process of being rebuilt to a greater height and strength. The typhoon demonstrated the vital need for this reinforcement at the same time as it destroyed much of the work in progress.

The flooding meant that rice fields which had just been rehabilitated with lime and phosphate after the last sea flooding were now full of salt again. This would mean low yields for several crops to come – and severe food shortages for Ky Anh as a whole.

This typhoon was rather exceptional. No local people died and few were injured. Structural damage was limited: 1,300 houses had collapsed, representing only two per cent of the district's houses. But the overall figures hide the misery of the people most affected by the typhoon. Even two weeks later the people of Ky Ha, a village which bore the brunt of the storm, were still struggling to recover from their traumatic experience.

Together we can make it happen. The whole community rallies round to fill the breach in the dyke.

KEITH BERNSTEIN

Nguyen Van Tu and his wife Lan had just finished rebuilding their house. A simple two-room structure with a thatched roof, its mud walls were still wet to the touch. Tu described the night of the typhoon. 'There was a mighty wind and the sea started to rise with great speed – within half an hour everywhere was flooded. All the animals in the village drowned – there was nothing we could do to save them. Nor could we save any of the things in our house. All we could do when we saw how the sea was rising was to pick up our children and set out into the darkness towards dry land. I had to force my way through water that was up to my neck in places, carrying both our two boys who were crying in terror.'

Once on dry land, Tu and Lan had immediately started building a temporary hut in which they could spend the night, demonstrating an

The day after the storm, Ky Anh starts to rebuild.

amazing self-reliance and resilience in the face of adversity. At least Tu and Lan are strong enough to start again. The future is altogether more doubtful for 68-year-old Hiec; all that remained of her house next door was a solitary wooden chest in the middle of what used to be the floor, somehow a more poignant sight than if there had been nothing left at all.

But in the long term, what all the villagers of Ky Ha needed was a stronger dyke that could protect them from flooding in future. When Tu was asked what he most needed, he said immediately 'Help to build a better dyke'.

Postcript: *Two months after Typhoon Becky had caused such devastation, engineers from Hanoi Water Resources University and Oxfam visited the site and carried out a careful assessment of the problems of resisting typhoon damage. By the end of 1990 a new, stronger dyke design had been drawn up, and checked by engineers from Britain's Hydraulics Research Institute. After training for local technicians and workteam leaders in basic construction techniques, 3,000 people from the local communes set to work, assisted by nine bulldozers, to rebuild the huge, 17-kilometre-long earth embankment. Soil was collected in baskets from nearby fields and carried to the site to be compacted by machines. The inner slope was planted with grass and the seaward slope covered with large, carefully-placed rocks, to protect it from the battering of the waves.*

Less than a year later, after about a million days of work by local people, the new dyke was completed, ready to protect the livelihoods of 5,000 families from the worst effects of future typhoons.

From Agent Orange to eroding earth

Over two million Vietnamese were killed and a further five million injured – 60 per cent of them children under 16 – during the long struggle against the French and the Americans. In addition, Vietnam sustained devastating environmental damage. Vietnam was the first country to be subjected to major ecological warfare. Half of the forest area in South Vietnam was seriously damaged and five per cent totally destroyed. In 1966 the US army began major land-clearing operations, with bulldozers flattening large areas of forest.

Between 1961 and 1974, American planes dropped 72 million litres of herbicides, much of it on South Vietnam's forests in order to strip the trees of their leaves so that the Vietnamese guerillas could not use the forests as their hiding place. Over 200,000 hectares of forest were completely destroyed by herbicides and defoliants, as were hundreds of thousands of hectares of crops. Most of the mangrove swamps in South Vietnam were also completely devastated.

The potent dioxin-based 'Agent Orange' was the most commonly used defoliant. Its low solubility means that dioxin is still present at dangerous levels in the soil in many parts of southern Vietnam, leaving the land unproductive 25 years after it was originally sprayed.

The effects of the war continue to cause major problems for the Vietnamese. Unexploded munitions and debris cause serious or fatal injuries to peasants and foresters; rank grass has replaced hectares of forest where chemicals were sprayed; children are born with deformities and abnormalities caused by the dioxins still lingering in the environment; the forests and fields are covered with bomb craters; and 20 per cent of the tidal mangrove swamps have not regenerated despite years of replanting.

But Vietnam's forests continue to be rapidly depleted despite the Government's ambitious replanting scheme. In 1943 Vietnam still had 44 per cent of its original forest cover; by the early 1980s it had been reduced to 23 per cent. A great number of trees were cut down in State forestry logging operations. Vietnamese scientists estimate that over 200,000 hectares per year are still being lost as a result of clearances by the State Forestry Enterprise, unplanned agricultural clearance, forest fires, and the collection of fuelwood.

The forest cover in Vietnam's mountains is essential to maintain the fragile layer of topsoil, soil it has taken thousands of years to produce. But every year now Vietnam's rivers are washing away tons of fertile soil from the deforested mountains out into the sea. Soil erosion now threatens 13 million hectares of open lands and denuded hills – some 40 per cent of Vietnam's total land area.

This much-needed fertile soil causes problems for the country's waterways. It silts up irrigation channels, reducing their efficiency, and shortens the useful life of dams and reservoirs. Da Nhim Lake, an important source of hydro-electric power, is so silted up that it no longer has enough water to maintain power-generating capacity

BEN FAWCETT

during the dry season.

Air and water pollution are also becoming a major concern in Vietnam's urban centres of Hanoi, Haiphong and Ho Chi Minh City. These are the familiar environmental problems associated with population increase and economic development. Toxic gases, lead and mineral dust are causing serious pollution in industrial zones. The discharge of heavily polluted waste water into water sources used for domestic and agricultural purposes is an increasing hazard.

Vietnam's problem is not its lack of awareness of the environmental dangers facing the country but the political will actually to do something about them. Indian ecologist Anil Agarwal, who recently studied Vietnam's environmental problems closely, concluded: 'while what ought to be done in Vietnam is well understood, the real problem is to get it done. The main problem

The bare hills of the far north. Primary forest has been cleared and cash crops planted in place of the trees. In the foreground is the Red River: soil washed down from the steep slopes is carried out to sea and lost forever.

remains the bureaucratic system.' But protecting the environment costs money, and Vietnam's economic isolation and lack of resources have also been a major reason why the Government has failed to get things done.

The conservation crusader

'If current trends in environmental degradation are allowed to continue unchecked,' says an official government strategy paper on national conservation, 'it is predicted that soon after 2000 AD there will be no natural forests left in the country.' The report's author, Professor Vo Quy, Dean of Biology at Hanoi University, persuaded the Government to adopt a major replanting scheme several years ago. 'Vietnam's goal is to organise the planting of a minimum of 200,000 hectares of trees annually. The re-greening of Vietnam is the biggest challenge facing the country since reunification.' He smiles disarmingly as he says this, as if confident that he can make things happen.

According to Vo Quy, 100 years of French colonialism and 30 years of war have destroyed Vietnam's environment. An ornithologist by training, Vo Quy has worked on environmental issues for over 20 years. During the war he took scientists into the battle zones in South Vietnam to monitor environmental damage. He has earned an international reputation for his work, and was awarded a gold medal by the World Wildlife Fund for his efforts to promote international co-operation.

'Vietnam's deforestation has had a devastating effect on the country,' says Vo Quy. 'Floods have intensified and become very dangerous as a result of Vietnam's impaired ecological balance. This imbalance worries me greatly, and I would like to see an increase in Vietnam's forest cover to 50 per cent, but at least 30 per cent as a minimum. When the ecology of an area is repaired by tree planting, the wild life returns and can be a useful economic resource. There is a close link between conservation and development. They must go hand in hand.'

Vo Quy is particularly pleased with his efforts to organise a sanctuary for Sarich's crane, which had been abundant in Vietnam but had come close to extinction from the effect of bombs, napalm and herbicides. In 1985, he heard that a small group of cranes had returned to the Mekong Delta. After visiting the area, and confirming their reappearance, he convinced the local people of the need to organise a sanctuary.

'We created a sanctuary of 5,000 hectares of wetlands and replanted the forest. After a year, the crane population had grown to 100, after two years it had grown to 400 and after three years to over 1,000. This even surprised me, but shows what can be done when scientists co-operate with local people at grassroots level.

Recovering environmental balance is not only important for the Vietnamese nation,' says Vo Quy, 'it is essential for the survival of the world.'

BEN FAWCETT

Small farmstead, Ky Anh. Traditional farming methods work in harmony with the environment.

Professor Vo Quy.

CHRIS BRAZIER

The ecological triangle

'What we have been doing for centuries is only now attracting the attention of outsiders,' says Doanh, a farmer in Ky Thinh commune. The mainstay of the Vietnamese household economy has traditionally been an integrated system consisting of garden (vuon), fishpond (ao) and livestock (chung). VAC is the backbone of household food supply.

On both sides of the national highway running from Hanoi to Ho Chi Minh City lie home-gardens allotted to farmers by the District. This local resettlement scheme was introduced in order to reduce pressure on fields at lower elevations, as well as to bring scrub land into more productive use. A year ago, Doanh and her family of four began work on their allotment of 300 square metres of poor red soil.

Diversification and minimising risks are the cornerstones of subsistence agriculture. While still working on her 500 square metres of co-operative paddy-land, Doanh decided to give her personal home-garden much of her attention. She edged the plot with mud walls to stop soil being washed away, and planted sea-pine and eucalyptus around the edges to provide fuel-wood in the future. Underneath these trees she grows tea and tobacco. She planted jackfruit for its fruit and timber, and, around the bomb crater that could later be made into a fishpond, sweet potatoes, squash, beans and chillies are growing. Doanh has also planted ginger, garlic onions, lemon-grass, betel, lettuce and pineapple near her house. Two rows of bananas have been sown and taro is growing near the family well, as it needs a lot of water.

Thieu Thi Quy and her pig. Oxfam supports a pig-breeding project in Ky Anh.

CHRIS BRAZIER

A pig-sty has been built next to the house, and a dozen chickens share a shed with a cow. 'I am too poor to keep a buffalo,' says Doanh, 'they're costly and they eat a lot. I didn't even have enough money to buy a pig, but fortunately the Women's Union provided me with a sow. The Union provides some feed and a veterinary service, including insemination. I have to return ten piglets to the Union over the next five years, which shouldn't be too difficult.'

The home-garden and the chickens provide for half the food needs of Doanh's family. Vegetable waste and rice-straw feed the pig. The cow is taken by one of the children to graze on public land. The manure from the pig, cow and chickens is used as fertiliser both for the vegetables and the rice crop. Doanh believes that chicken manure makes chillies extra hot, just the way she likes them. She doesn't yet have spare money to invest in fingerling fish, and her children are as yet too small to help with digging out the proposed fishpond. That is a plan for the future – and will complete her own ecological triangle.

Gods under Marx

Vietnam is identified by the outside world with Marxism and thus with atheism, yet religion has played a major part in its history, both ancient and recent, and continues to exercise an influence over the lives of ordinary people.

The country's main religion has evolved out of a fusion of three separate spiritual strands – Buddhism, Taoism and Confucianism – with ingredients of animism and ancestor worship thrown in. People are most likely to call themselves Buddhists, and Buddhism was the official state religion of Vietnam as long ago as the twelfth century. But in practice, Buddhist purists have fought for centuries to overcome the popular predilection for belief in a pantheon of deities who can help out in everyday life. Even the most sophisticated, urbanised Vietnamese are quite likely to have a small shrine in their home, dedicated to their ancestors, and to seek their ancestors' blessing on, for example, a new marriage. This ancient tradition was of particular value after Liberation, as people who had been politically divided for 30 years could find unity in their respect for common ancestors.

Vietnamese Buddhism hit the world headlines in 1963 when the American-sponsored President Diem of South Vietnam, himself a Catholic, started a campaign of vicious repression. Diem resented the campaigns of Buddhist priests against his regime's corruption and authoritarianism but his clampdown went too far: a priest burned himself to death in full view of US television cameras. This helped persuade the US to back the coup that deposed Diem.

This history of resistance has helped to ease the relationship between Buddhists and the Vietnamese Communists. According to Phan Chau Toan, now 75, a devout Buddhist who has run a herbal-medicine centre in Danang for over 40 years, things have actually been a lot easier since the Communist takeover of the South. 'Of course it is necessary to show the authorities the proper respect when, for example, we have someone coming here from another province for treatment. But we always do this and as a result they have always shown us respect.'

Toan's own living room is a testimony to his faith – as well as some elegant carved furniture it contains a large Buddhist shrine in a recess high on one wall; on another wall is the usual portrait of Ho Chi Minh. 'The actual work of the clinic,' he continues, 'is much easier now than it was under the Diem regime when they imposed all kinds of bureaucratic procedures and forbade the collection of the roots and herbs we depend on – the Americans had told them these were poisonous.'

Christianity was brought to Vietnam by Catholic missionaries from Europe in the early seventeenth century. The overtly Catholic nature of the Diem regime reflected the fact that Catholics had been repressed by the Communists in northern Vietnam: when the country was divided in 1954 around 800,000 Catholics, including 80 per cent of the priesthood, left to live in South Vietnam. This inevitably meant that Catholics approached the Liberation of the South by the Communists in 1975 with a good deal of apprehension. But, given that between eight and ten per cent of

BEN FAWCETT

Buddhist cave shrine.

Pagoda on an island in the river.

JILL ARACE

Vietnamese consider themselves Catholic, the Communists could not afford to be too heavy-handed.

Nguyen Thanh Cong and Nguyen Nghi, editors of the Catholic newspaper *Cong Giáo va Dan Toc*, explain what has happened since. 'Before Liberation, the Communists considered Catholicism to be an instrument of imperialism – after that they had to learn how to live with it. We were still able to attend church as before; we basically had freedom of worship though, of course, we could no longer parade through the streets without permission. Priests from the army of the old regime were put in re-education camps. And there was overt discrimination – Catholics weren't allowed to study in certain university faculties such as medicine and politics, and this only changed in 1986; Catholics are still not allowed to become Party members. Because of that last rule we find ourselves in a unique position – every other paper has a Party member sitting in on the operation, but we escape that because there are no Catholics in the Party.

BEN FAWCETT

Christmas Eve, Roman Catholic Cathedral, Hanoi.

'Since 1986 the climate for free speech has certainly improved enormously. It is still normal for agents to sit listening to sermons, and the number of police has not noticeably diminished. But everyone can now express their ideas and even criticise, though it stops there – you can't organise or demonstrate, for example. We just printed an article which argued that religious freedom is a person's right rather than something given by the authorities. Before 1986 the phone lines would have been on fire but now the authorities don't seem to worry.

'Our own line at the paper is very much in sympathy with the Liberation Theology of Latin America and its identification with the poor. We wouldn't exactly call ourselves socialists but we recognise that our human goals are generally better served under socialism than under capitalism. A "third way" might be best of all but has yet to emerge. We need democratisation rather than democracy in Vietnam. The Communist Party has liberated Vietnam three times already and it must now do it a fourth time by sacrificing some of its own power, its privileges and monopolies.'

View from the hills

Go to any country in the world and you are likely to find its immigrant minorities in the urban ghettoes. But if you are looking for indigenous ethnic minorities who have maintained their own separate traditions you do better to head for the hills, as far away as possible from the centres of power and wealth.

Vietnam is no exception. Fully 87 per cent of the people in Vietnam are Kinh people – those we normally think of as Vietnamese. They dominate the rich rice-growing lands of the Deltas and the lowland plains. But there are 52 other ethnic groups in Vietnam – and nearly all of them can be found in the highlands that rise up to form the country's northern and western borders.

Here, through the centuries, they have maintained their own distinct languages and cultural practices. Different ethnic groups tend to live at different heights up the mountains. Some of them still wear traditional, colourful costumes – in other regions of South-East Asia 'hill tribes' closely related to these have become tourist attractions for Western visitors.

But not all of them can be so clearly identified by the outsider as a people apart. In the hills of northern Bac Thai province most of the people are from ethnic minorities, yet their dress differs little from that of the Kinh majority, and they farm in fields between the hills rather than depending on shifting cultivation. Their houses are often different in style – the Tay, for example, who form the largest of all the minorities in Vietnam, build impressive thatched homes raised high above the ground on stilts. Yet when you talk to people here they seem to see little contradiction between being Tay and being Vietnamese. It makes you remember that Ho Chi Minh and his guerillas spent years living among the minorities in these northern hills – that the Vietnamese Communist Party began its journey to power from here.

KEITH BERNSTEIN

KEITH BERNSTEIN

Vietnam's ethnic minorities live in a world apart. The people here are Hmong and live in Sa Pa district near the Chinese border.

Like most nations, Vietnam tends to want to 'integrate' minorities into the mainstream – the 1980 constitution makes no provision for their special rights. While the Government talks about preserving the language and culture of minorities, there is actually much more emphasis on protecting 'the community of the Vietnamese nation'.

Mr Dan, who is Chair of the province's Phu Luong District, could be said to embody this approach to minorities. He has considerable power and status, despite not being a Kinh, nor even from the Tay people who form 60 per cent of his constituency. He is from the Dao minority, yet he seems almost devoid of pride in his traditional culture. He goes as far as to say that he does not think it is important that Dao language and culture are disappearing. Perhaps he has had to repudiate his background in order to reach his present position of power in a predominately Kinh society. He only identifies with his own ethnic origins at one point – when he pours scorn on the habitual assumption in Vietnam that deforestation in the hills, which is an ever-greater problem, is caused by the shifting agriculture of minority peoples. He points out that peoples like his own have learned how to live sustainably within their fragile environment – the real damage, here just as much as in the Amazon rainforest, is done by settlers from outside and by massive commercial logging operations.

Most ethnic-minority people would not share Mr Dan's feeling that traditional culture is unimportant; and the more remote the community, the more evident it is that 'integration' is not a sufficient answer. Sa Pa is just a stone's throw from the Chinese border; most of its people are from the Hmong minority. Here the majority are illiterate and child mortality rates are very high: life is hard. School attendance is poor, and is unlikely to improve while only 10 of the district's 200 teachers are from ethnic minorities.

Vietnam is a multi-cultural society with a rich diversity of peoples and languages. But its current approach to ethnic minorities will inevitably reduce that diversity in the future.

KEITH BERNSTEIN

Tet – the celebration of the lunar new year

Tet is the most important festival in the Vietnamese year, celebrating the passage of the old year and the start of a new one. Preparations last several days, as houses are scrupulously cleaned, and special food, such as crystallised coconut, tamarind seeds, kumquats and ginger, is bought and prepared to offer to visiting family and friends.

The most important culinary ritual is the cooking of *banh chung*. This is a cake made of sticky rice, mung beans and fatty pork, wrapped in banana leaves. Cooking takes a long time, as the rice has to be soaked for 24 hours and the cake is then boiled for two days. A charming legend explains why such ordinary ingredients are used: long ago, a king of Vietnam sent his children to different countries to seek recipes for a national dish. The older children travelled far and wide and returned with exotic and expensive dishes, but the youngest, unable to travel, stayed at home and dreamt of *banh chung* being made from the foodstuffs she ate every day. Her father was so impressed with the dish's simplicity and cheapness that he decreed that it should become the celebration food for Tet.

As the New Year approaches, the graves of the family ancestors are whitewashed and shrines prepared in Vietnamese homes, with offerings of food and incense sticks. Debts must be paid off, and sweeping and scrubbing of the home continues until midnight, to drive out the bad spirits and make way for the good ones. Once the New Year has arrived, no cleaning is done for several days, lest the good spirits be driven away and bad luck strike the family for the rest of the year.

Flowers are an important part of the celebrations, and street flower markets spring up all over towns and villages. Houses are decorated with branches of peach blossom to ward off bad spirits, and little kumquat bushes as a symbol of fruitfulness. Tet is a very colourful time as people wander the streets with armfuls of flowers.

Midnight is greeted with a deafening crescendo of firecrackers – a sound that will continue for days, until supplies run out. Then the visits to relatives and friends begin. The choice of the first person to cross a threshold after midnight is very important; they must be of good character, in good health and not owing any money. All guests are welcomed with food and drink. The cheerful bustle of families, dressed in their finest clothes, travelling around towns and cities and across the country to their family homes, continues for several days. Meanwhile, no work is done and shops and markets stay firmly closed. Only after about two weeks of festivities does normal life resume, and people face the challenges of another year.

BEN FAWCETT

Bland, state-controlled media cannot blunt the appetite for news. Outside the main office of the* Hanoi Moi *newspaper.

The democracy taboo

Democracy is always a loaded concept – and it is bound to be so in Vietnam, which had to endure a long and terrible war with the US on the grounds that its Communist leaders were 'enemies of democracy'. Vietnam's Government remains unequivocal that only one political party is allowed, and the General Secretary of the Communist Party is the country's leader just as its Politburo is the country's executive body. The National Assembly does little more than rubber-stamp the Politburo's decisions. And this in a country where less than three per cent of the population are members of the Communist Party.

Yet, for all that, Vietnam's political structure does allow elements of democracy. Each local commune, district and province is run by a People's Council which is elected by universal suffrage every five years. The People's Councils, in turn, elect an executive People's Committee, of only a few members, to carry out their policies and to administer the area under their jurisdiction from day to day. People's Council members do not have to belong to the Party, though in practice they usually do. This would mean nothing if local government were simply implementing a line from Hanoi. But it is widely agreed in Vietnam that an old saying about the edicts of the Emperor applies nowadays to those of the Communist Party – that they are 'interpreted' to fit local conditions in a way that can render the decree unrecognisable by the time it reaches the village.

There is plenty of evidence to suggest that the radical change of direction represented by *doi moi* was itself inspired by grassroots criticism of the centrally controlled economy and stagnant bureaucracy.

Doi moi's effects have not been purely economic – there is no question that there has been a much freer atmosphere in Vietnam since 1986. Whereas ordinary people used to be afraid to say what they thought for fear of local informers or the secret police, a legacy in part of the need to protect sensitive information during 36 years of war, now they are much more ready to speak their minds – even to total strangers coming from the West, with whom any contact at all was previously forbidden. Yet there are still limits and people are used to censoring themselves: again and again they will trail off,

BEN FAWCETT

Day of the firecrackers: Tet brings its own commercial opportunities.

BEN FAWCETT

BEN FAWCETT

***Left:* Everyone buys flowers to celebrate Tet, and street flower markets spring up in every town and village. The little kumquat bushes symbolise fruitfulness.**

***Below:* Waiting for a bite. Fish is a very important source of protein in the Vietnamese diet.**

KEITH BERNSTEIN

Left: Memorial at My Lai, south of Danang, in memory of the victims of the massacre which took place during the war with the US.

SARAH LOCK

A Buddhist ceremony at the Vinh Nghiem Pagoda, built in 1964, the largest and most modern in Ho Chi Minh City.

Hmong grandmother and grandchild.

BEN FAWCETT

Red Dao women, at a market in Sa Pa in northern Vietnam, wearing their colourful, everyday dress.

KEITH BERNSTEIN

saying something like 'This is getting dangerously political...'

Between 1986 and 1989, the policy of *doi moi* allowed a good deal of free political debate and comment on human-rights issues. Articles in newspapers spoke out freely against instances of corruption by local or national officials and uncovered examples of unjust detention, or ill-treatment by police. But after 1990, this new freedom suffered a setback; open criticism in the press diminished, and some dissidents were arrested, among them the well-known woman novelist Duong Thu Huong, who was detained for several months. She is a former Communist Party member, whose novels were critical of many aspects of party rule.

In general, the Government has been much keener to promote economic reform than any political change which might threaten the Communist Party's 'leading role'. But as society becomes more open and fluid in response to the new liberal approach to economics, some people are inevitably starting to expect and demand more freedom of speech.

This is predictable enough in the South, where there are thousands of people who fought actively against Communist rule. But even in Hanoi there is mounting impatience with the Party's reluctance to consider political reform, at least in student and intelligentsia circles. One dissident explains: 'We need other political parties apart from the Communists – we are all talking about pluralism now, at least in private. We need democracy as well as dollars here in Vietnam.'

BEN FAWCETT

Ho, Engels and Marx preside over this meeting in Nghe Tinh province.

Such talk of multi-party democracy is still taboo. The Government is prepared to countenance calls for more democracy – the term is so elastic that it can be interpreted as making the Party more responsive to the people. But it will not tolerate any mention of other political parties. For the moment there is no mass movement likely to force it to think otherwise. Yet there are the first stirrings of popular dissent. On Vietnam's National Day in 1991, leaflets calling for the overthrow of the Government were distributed in Hanoi, in the northern province of Hai Hung and the southern province of Tien Giang.

Pressure for change is building up even within the Party itself. In the words of a dissident journalist: 'We must democratise the Party and the social organisations under the Party. There must be more democratic and civil rights; increased freedom of expression, freedom to write, freedom of speech.' (Outspoken comments like this have led to his expulsion from the Communist Party.)

Behind the scenes of the Politburo a fierce debate went on in 1990 and 1991 between reformers and conservatives – with General Secretary Nguyen Van Linh somewhere between the two. At the Seventh Party Congress in June 1991 – the first Congress to be held since the one which set *doi moi* in motion – the personalities involved in this battle changed. Linh retired as leader and was replaced by the former Prime Minister Do Muoi, a moderate. In general, the changes seemed to indicate continued cautious reform.

It is hard to predict how Vietnam may change in the future. Will the Communist Party eventually have to accept greater democracy, free speech and even competing political parties? Or will it reaffirm its central role? Events in Eastern Europe have shown how rapidly and unexpectedly radical political change can overturn monolithic governments; and Vietnam is facing similar pressures after the failure of state planning has led to a liberalisation of the economy. But even outspoken critics of the Government like Dr Duong Quynh Hoa accept the need for political stability as Vietnam tries to change.

'I believe democracy and respect for human rights are necessary things,' she says. 'A country can't be built without them. And if the Revolution succeeded, it was because it proclaimed a fundamental human right – to be free and independent. But if you ask me are we going to have political pluralism here in five years, then I have to say I don't know. Honestly, I'm in favour of pluralism. But honestly, too, I'm a bit afraid of it. You know why? Because the bulk of the Vietnamese population really aren't politically aware. I have discussed it with the leaders. I've said "We have to have democracy. At the moment we don't have democracy. But that doesn't mean just any old kind of democracy. It doesn't mean anarchy." And when a people has never lived democratically and you suddenly open up you run the risk of anarchy.'

Her words are echoed by Catholic newspaper editors Nguyen Thanh Cong and Nguyen Nghi. 'We're not necessarily of the view that a multi-party system would be the right thing here at the moment. Look at the convulsions in Eastern Europe, where they tried to switch over immediately and became unstable – you can be sure things would be worse in a poor country like Vietnam. We have to change bit by bit. But we'll arrive in the end in our own Vietnamese way – which usually means waiting a very, very long time for what you want.'

The outlaw state

Two of this book's recurring themes have been the legacy of the American War and the US-led embargo on trade and aid with Vietnam. It would be easy to assume that the second was part and parcel of the first – but, ostensibly at least, it was not.

For the first few years after the war, Vietnam benefited from international aid. A few of those aid-givers have maintained a presence in Vietnam right through to the present day: the Swedish Government, for example, along with various United Nations agencies. By all but these, however, Vietnam has been considered an outlaw state ever since its invasion of Cambodia in 1978.

Why, after just three years of peace at the end of four decades of violence, did Vietnam invade a neighbour and install a government it considered more suitable? Does this not smack of militaristic expansionism?

Well, possibly. But no-one could deny that the Vietnamese were provoked. Cambodian troops had attacked across their southern border repeatedly between 1975 and 1978, causing constant disruption and thousands of Vietnamese casualties. It is clear that this border conflict was a prime cause for the Vietnamese invasion.

But it might reasonably be asked why retaliation should have involved marching to Phnom Penh and deposing the Cambodian Government. One answer is to consider what Vietnam's soldiers found when they crossed the border. Hardly anyone realised, until the Vietnamese invaded, the scale of the genocide that had been inflicted on the Cambodian people by Pol Pot's Khmer Rouge government. The Vietnamese found cities deserted; mass graves full of human skulls; a nation shattered by the extinction of more than a million of its citizens. Cambodians have a traditional distrust of Vietnam but after the unimaginable nightmare they had endured for the previous three and a half years, it is small wonder that most of them saw the invading troops, at first, as liberators.

The deposing of Pol Pot's government, in itself, could be considered a service to humanity; instead, Vietnam has paid a high price for its actions in 1978, and its continued support for the government it installed in Phnom Penh. The Vietnamese may well consider that they lost an incalculable amount as a result of their presence in Cambodia: the occupying force (320,000-strong at its peak) drained the nation of its fittest young people; and the international embargo froze Vietnam into stagnant isolation.

If the country in general now has reason to wonder whether these sacrifices have been worthwhile, so too do the young Vietnamese who actually served in the army. Long, for instance, who now works on the railways, was conscripted in 1980 at the age of 20 and spent five years in Cambodia without a single period of home leave.

'I can't tell you how difficult life was there – I saw many friends die. Yes, I killed people: when I was face to face with the enemy I had no option if I was to stay alive.'

At first Long was idealistic about the war against the Khmer Rouge. 'I felt it was my duty to serve in the People's Army. I felt

KEITH BERNSTEIN

that now we had achieved our independence we had a responsibility to help a neighbouring country which was not so fortunate. What do I feel now?'

He pauses, as if wondering whether he dares say it. 'Well, I think the Cambodian War cost this country too dear.'

Long's successors in the army of occupation were required to stay in Cambodia until September 1989 when the last contingent was withdrawn. Since then Vietnam's desire to bring about an internationally acceptable peace agreement has been intense – and ultimately this has overcome their understandable reluctance to accept the Khmer Rouge as legitimate partners in the settlement.

The signing of the Cambodian peace accord in October 1991 was as momentous for Vietnam as for its neighbour: it should mark the beginning of the end of Vietnam's long isolation. As if to underscore the point, the accord was followed soon after by US Secretary of State James Baker's statement that his country was at last willing to talk seriously about resuming relations with Vietnam – and thus bringing the embargo to an end.

The Cambodian problem has in many ways been convenient for the US Government, allowing it to maintain its frosty attitude to Vietnam for reasons other than its own military defeat in Indochina. For Americans, the Vietnam War represents a deep and persistent national trauma. The experience of defeat has marked the national consciousness and the loss of thousands of young American lives is a continuing grief. One sign of this is the rooted belief in the existence, somewhere in Vietnam, of US prisoners of war – the 'Missing in Action' or MIAs. It is hard to see what Vietnam would have had to gain by holding back prisoners; but the MIAs issue has been a formidable barrier to normal relations.

The US played a major role in the Cambodian peace process; but an even more important force was China, which backed the Khmer Rouge faithfully throughout. The Chinese Government may not have been as appalled as the rest of the world by their Cambodian ally's past record, but their support had much more to do with distrust of Vietnam than with enthusiasm for the Khmer Rouge.

China and Vietnam have a long history of antipathy. Vietnam was actually part of China for a thousand years, until the tenth century. Since then China has continued to see its southern neighbour as a legitimate region of influence. General Giap, who commanded the Vietnamese army against both the French and the Americans (and received substantial support from Mao Zedong's Communists), describes relations with China as 'a family affair: we're brothers. But China sees Vietnam as the younger brother and gets angry when we defy them.'

The involvement in Cambodia was seen as just such an act of defiance, and China duly invaded Vietnam in February 1979 as 'punishment'. After a month of heavy fighting the Chinese were forced back across the border but, as they withdrew, they blew up everything they could behind them: four major provincial capitals and hundreds of villages were demolished, and a quarter of a million Vietnamese found themselves homeless.

The Cambodian peace accord therefore holds the promise of better relations on this front too. At the Seventh Congress of the

BEN FAWCETT

Every town and district in Vietnam has its war-cemetery for those who died fighting in the American War. This one is in Nghe Tinh Province.

Communist Party in 1991 Vietnam changed its leadership, and one of the casualties was Nguyen Co Thach, who had been Foreign Minister ever since the reunion of North and South in 1975. Thach was consistently hostile to China, preferring to make overtures to the West, and his removal was seen in part as a gesture towards Beijing. Sure enough, plans were immediately laid for a summit meeting between the new head of the Communist Party, Do Muoi, and his Chinese counterpart, Jiang Zemin, which took place at the end of the year.

Some Western observers view the thaw in this East Asian Cold War with disquiet, seeing a closer relationship between Vietnam's leaders and the hard-line Communist regime in China as a threat to political and economic liberalisation in Vietnam. But, remembering that Vietnam has also applied to sign the Bali Treaty as a step to joining with its capitalist neighbours in the Association of South East Asian Nations (ASEAN), it is possible that Vietnam is simply trying to make friends at both ends of the political spectrum, to secure the peace it so badly needs.

Reaching out to the world

You can't spend long in Vietnam without coming across some painful reminder of the war against the US. The physical evidence is less obvious these days: the rusting metal from destroyed tanks or aeroplanes has been put to good use; the bomb craters have been converted into fishponds; and even the areas of the South which were so ravaged by the American use of chemical defoliants are now finally beginning to recover. The capital Hanoi escaped major bombing damage, with the result that the historic 36 streets at its centre, around the Lake of the Restored Sword, still stand – quietly elegant, though crumbling and sorely in need of repair.

No, these days the painful reminders come from people. Almost everyone above the age of 25 lost someone in the War; almost everyone would have a sad story to tell if you probed deep enough. Take Le Van Dang, a local official in the Mekong Delta town of Tan An, who repeats the Party line on food production in the area until he is asked about his wartime experiences – he was originally a teacher in Hanoi but was ordered into the South to work undercover as a 'political educator'.

'Of course it was hard to be away from my family for eight years, not even able to write or receive letters. But there was no time in those days even to think of family life. In front of me there was always the question "death or life". Like all Vietnamese, though, I wanted to live in peace and return to my family. When I met my parents and children again after all that time there are no words to describe the emotions. We were all crying, of course. On the day I left the North my children were so small that they could not remember what I looked like and it took three days for them to stop being wary of me.'

He pauses and looks uncertain, then seems to take a decision and continues. 'But I don't want to hide anything from you. The fact is that while I was away my wife had married another man – I suppose she had thought I was dead. So I ended up coming back down here to live and work. No, I'm not in contact with her any more.'

The War left the Vietnamese with deep scars. Like Dang, they are more interested in getting on with life than in dwelling on the past – everyone, from the highest government official to the peasant farmer from an ethnic minority up in the hills, talks about setting the country on a new road that will offer it a brighter future.

Yet Vietnam has been unable to shake off the legacy of the War, mainly because of its extreme economic and political isolation. After reunification in 1975, Vietnam's leaders (perhaps naively) were banking on Western aid in reconstructing the country – and specifically for three billion dollars in war reparations which had been promised to them by President Nixon. Instead, in the wake of the Cambodian invasion, they

The scars of war run deeper for Phuong than most. He lost both legs in a mine explosion and now makes his living on Danang's streets as a bike mechanic.

CHRIS BRAZIER

were faced with the international embargo on trade and aid which is still in place today.

After World War Two a devastated Western Europe was enabled to rebuild by a massive injection of US aid under the Marshall Plan. Without that aid, European recovery would have been infinitely slower and standards of living would have remained much lower for decades. Yet Vietnam, which had more bombs dropped on it between 1964 and 1973 than did the whole world during the Second World War, has received next to no Western aid to help it rebuild. It has relied instead on the Soviet bloc – but now even that help has evaporated completely, as old priorities have given way to new in Moscow.

As a result, Vietnam's isolation and economic crisis have increased even as its policies have become more liberal and outward-looking – its conversion to market economics and financial discipline has been lauded to the skies by the International Monetary Fund but no cash or concrete benefit has yet been forthcoming. The World Bank says 'It is quite remarkable that these results have been achieved with little external assistance' – but that does not make future assistance any less necessary. There has been a very different response by the West to the countries of Eastern Europe after their rejection of state socialist economics.

There is no doubt that the Vietnamese Government is earnest in its desire to enter the global market economy. It can even seem too eager, as with the member of the state committee to encourage foreign investment who says: 'The only thing we are trying to learn from our neighbours is what deal they are offering the multinationals, so that we can undercut them. We want to offer foreign companies more profit, more freedom to operate, so that we can attract as much of their money here as possible.'

Even the World Bank seems a little worried about the impact this desperation to attract foreign investment might have on the future development of the economy. 'The development of indigenous entrepreneurs and firms can be hampered,' it says, 'if the economy comes to be dominated by foreign firms.'[1]

There are other worries about the headlong dash towards a market economy, primarily that Vietnam's hitherto admirable health and education services will suffer and that a gap will open up between rich and poor. A recent report on the economy by the United Nations Development Programme is explicit about this: 'The prevailing degree of equality in Vietnamese society deserves particular emphasis. The reduction of overall inequality, the broad-based provision of basic social services, particularly in health and education, and the limited differentials between rural and urban standards of living represent significant achievements... A fair system of land distribution and the maintenance of a health and education system that provides widespread access should be defended as important assets whatever the particular choice of economic instruments to be used in promoting growth.'[2]

[1] Vietnam: Stabilization and Structural Reforms, World Bank internal report, April 1990.

[2] Report on the Economy of Vietnam, United Nations Development Programme, December 1990.

KEITH BERNSTEIN

Facing the future together: lovers beside the lake in Lenin Park, Hanoi.

But for the moment, at least, even people who have spent their whole lives making equality the top social and political priority see economic growth as more important. Huu Tho was among Ho Chi Minh's soldiers liberating Hanoi from the French in 1954 and is now deputy editor of the Party newspaper *Nhan Dan*. When asked if he is worried about a gap opening up between rich and poor he replies: 'Yes I am. But it's not a simple matter. I've just visited a woman, for instance, who owns 52 cows. These produce 300 litres of milk daily and she collects another 300 litres from her neighbours then sells the lot to a factory producing condensed milk. She employs seven labourers on an average wage of 300,000 dong a month [about £40, or three times what ordinary Vietnamese consider a decent living wage].

'In the old days she wouldn't have been allowed to do this because we would have been afraid of her getting rich and exploiting people. But her work seems to benefit everyone. Why should we oppose her? At this stage in our development we actually need some people who have the art of management to get a little richer.

'If you'd talked to me five years ago I'd have given you the opposite view. But I now think we shouldn't allow our concern for the poor to put obstacles in the way of the rich. In my view the Government should only control the big industries like power and construction. And there is no more time for propaganda.'

The view you get in the fields and streets may be less considered than Huu Tho's but it is just as unequivocal. One perspective on the country's current plight would be to say that Vietnam won the war against impossible odds, only to lose the peace. Yet no-one who took their cue from the Vietnamese people could possibly see things so negatively. Far from feeling a sense of defeat, they are full of enthusiasm for the changes sweeping through their country. They see their fresh start as a great adventure. And despite all the poverty and the problems, they have such energy and ability that it is not so far-fetched to imagine some kind of economic miracle taking place here. Remember the courage, commitment and skill that the Vietnamese showed in defeating the greatest military power on earth and then suppose all of that focused on commerce and trade, on making headway in the global marketplace – their economy is surely bound to take off.

But they have to be given a fair chance. The outside world's view of the Vietnamese people as hostile and isolationist could not be further from the truth. On the contrary, they are painfully keen to look outwards, excited by the idea that they might at last be able to cast off their pariah status and make friends with all the world. If the Vietnamese people have a single message for us it is this, in the words of Toan from Danang: 'The most fervent hope of everyone, me included, is that we can now live in peace. Voilà, c'est tout.'

KEITH BERNSTEIN

Oxfam in Vietnam

OXFAM has worked in Vietnam for many years – helping to resettle refugees and distributing medical supplies to victims of conflict in both the north and south of the country during the war years. Since 1975 Oxfam has worked closely with government officials to promote development activities with poor communities.

A large grant – nearly a quarter of a million pounds – was made in 1980 when Typhoon Joe wreaked havoc in the northern provinces of the Red River Delta. Oxfam responded with relief supplies which were distributed by Aidrecep, the committee charged with overseeing aid programmes in Vietnam.

Guided by the Government's development priorities, Oxfam's programme has focused on supporting food production and disaster prevention in the poorest areas of Vietnam, assisting with the small-scale manufacture of basic consumer goods and helping to make improvements in the health system.

In 1988, when Vietnam began to open up to foreign visitors, Oxfam approached the authorities for permission to open an office. Two years later Oxfam's office was established in Hanoi, with a staff of one expatriate and several Vietnamese. Oxfam now spends about half a million pounds each year in four of the poorest provinces of Vietnam.

Since then a number of similar non-governmental organisations (NGOs) from all over the world have established offices in Vietnam, and many others fund programmes from their headquarters. International NGOs work alongside the many agencies of the United Nations, and a gradually increasing number of Western government aid programmes.

Further reading

Beresford M. (1988), *Vietnam: politics, economics and society*, London: Pinter.

Burchett W. (1965), *Vietnam: inside story of the guerrilla war*, New York: International Publishers.

Evans G. and Rowley K. (1990, 2nd edition), *Red Brotherhood at War: Vietnam, Cambodia and Laos since 1975*, London: Verso.

Fitzgerald F. (1972), *Fire in the Lake*, Boston US: Atlantic, Little Brown.

Greene G. (1955), *The Quiet American*, London: Heinemann.

Grey A. (1983), *Saigon*, London: Pan.

Hitchcox L. (1990), *Vietnamese refugees in South East Asian Camps*, London: Macmillan.

Hodgkin T. (1981), *Vietnam: the revolutionary path*, London: Macmillan.

Karnow S. (1984), *Vietnam: a history*, London: Penguin.

Kemf E. (1990), *Month of Pure Light: the regreening of Vietnam*, London: The Women's Press.

Maclear M. (1981), *Vietnam: the ten thousand day war*, London: Eyre Methuen.

Mullin C. (1986), *Last Man out of Saigon*, London: Gollancz.

Snepp F. (1977), *Decent Interval*, New York: Random House.

Far Eastern Economic Review, weekly, Hong Kong.